Emotional Intelligence Business

Improve Emotional Intelligence at Work. Improve Leadership and Develop Your EQ. Unleash the Empath in You and Build Self Confidence

Benedict Daniel

Tables of Contents

Introduction 5

Chapter 1: Human Emotions in Business 7

Chapter 2: EQ Models Every Business Leader Need to Know 44

Chapter 3: Boost Your Emotional Intelligence 98

Chapter 4: Improve your leadership skills 143

Chapter 5: Master Time Management 170

Chapter 6: Build Self-Confidence 178

Conclusion 185

© **Copyright 2019 - All rights reserved.**

The content contained within this book may not be reproduced, duplicated or transmitted without direct written permission from the author or the publisher.

Under no circumstances will any blame or legal responsibility be held against the publisher, or author, for any damages, reparation, or monetary loss due to the information contained within this book, either directly or indirectly.

Legal Notice:

This book is copyright protected. It is only for personal use. You cannot amend, distribute, sell, use, quote or paraphrase any part, or the content within this book, without the consent of the author or publisher.

Disclaimer Notice:

Please note the information contained within this document is for educational and entertainment purposes only. All effort has been executed to present accurate, up to date, reliable, complete information. No warranties of any kind are declared or implied. Readers acknowledge that the author is not engaging in the rendering of legal, financial, medical or professional advice. The content within this book has been derived from various sources. Please consult a licensed professional before attempting any techniques outlined in this book.

By reading this document, the reader agrees that under no circumstances is the author responsible for any losses, direct or indirect, that are incurred as a result of the use of the information contained within this document, including, but not limited to, errors, omissions, or inaccuracies.

Introduction

When it comes to leadership, emotional intelligence is one of those major talking points. One that is true for sure is that it is a character that can be developed.

Emotional intelligence involves one's potential to recognize and regulate their emotions, while gathering the said emotions to have the best reaction as situations require. It also has to deal with the awareness and sensitivity of others emotions.

For that reason, emotional intelligence is a vital trait for everyone in an organization, especially for those who hold positions. A leader's emotional intelligence can have a huge impact over their relationships, how they control their teams, and how they interact with people in the workplace.

For leaders, having emotional intelligence is critical for success. Ask yourself, between a leader who shouts at people in an organization when under stress, and that one who stays in control of their emotions and calmly examines the situation. Of these two leaders, who is likely to take the company forward.

This book will review the traits of a leader with a high emotional intelligence. We shall look at ways to boost your emotional intelligence, and many more interesting topics. Keep reading to learn more.

Chapter 1: Human Emotions in Business

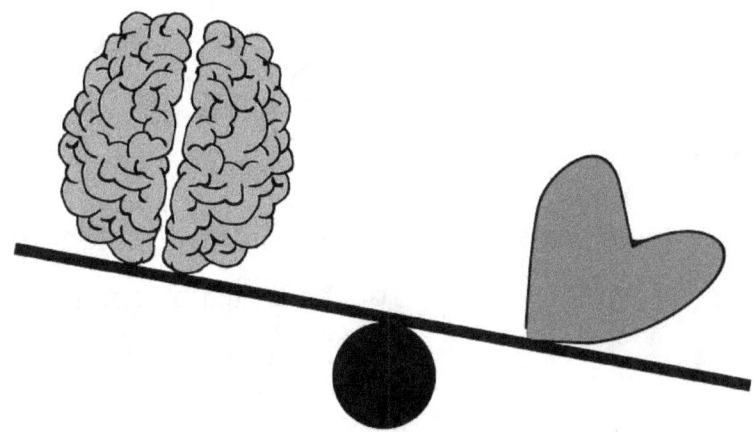

Your strongest emotions are connected to your strongest emotional experiences. How you will initially respond to current events is linked to those memories.

This is not just about your childhood. These memories are being created today. At work. In your business. By everyone on your team.

Past events that have a strong positive emotion are well recalled.

Negatives defeat positives.

Success in any business relies on our mastery of emotions. The reason is that whoever purchases what you are selling is doing so for emotional purposes. Emotions drive human action. Good feelings attract your customer closer to a sale while negative emotions make your customers purchase your product to calm their discomfort.

Our entire lives are a sequence of actions directed by the emotions of anger, fear, disgust, anticipation, joy, and sadness.

Every sale ever created was completed because the product activated the buyer through one or a combination of these eight fundamental emotions.

For example, a customer searching for movie CD's these days is a collector. He or she might be a big fan and wants to check the CD, the booklet, to see it in his or her collection at home. This individual may want to touch the product, to feel it. This customer is not shopping to watch the movie alone. He or she reacts to different emotions than the customer that wants to see a great film.

The latter customer can watch the same movie on stream and for cheap. However, because a lot of movie buffs have an emotional attachment to the physical CD provided at home, the CD market is essential. Paper books are another great example. Although it is cheaper and more practical to download a file and read a digital text on a laptop, and even tablet, paper books are still popular these days. The bottom line is, people don't purchase most things because it makes rational sense; they buy because they feel the need. To succeed, we must understand the emotions behind our customer's decision-making and align our design and production to develop what the customer wants.

The most successful businesses out there have all touched their esteemed clients' emotions. You might have already heard one of the most critical factors of success is to have a unique product that solves big problems for as many people as possible. Being the first to solve this problem and get discovered by your target audience is significant. If you are settling an important problem, they will want to use your product to solve their problem. What pushes these customers is not a desire for the product, but an emotional impulse to eliminate frustration. Most customers only want relief. We purchase food because eating is good, and we want food in the house to avoid frustration. Once we are relieved of frustration, we always brag to our friends and family.

Sharing the story of overcoming these challenges makes us feel good. These days, people express their joy and frustrations in social media to their networks of online friends.

None of this is new to most people. What is important is what happens before a product reaches the door and is available for the customer. Developers, designers, producers, and programmers all get confused with their own emotions trying to deliver a product a target audience wants. Companies whose design decisions concentrate on solving a dominant frustration win big.

Some years back, Google was not running ads, but many search engines preceded it. Before the emergence of Google, all search engines were slow and inefficient. They also had messed up interfaces. When Google emerged with a clean interface, powerful search algorithms, and speed, most people felt like they have found the Holy Grail. So much good. Therefore, people started to use Google Search and never looked back. This was the beginning of Google's success. The company saw the competition, learned the frustration of slow inefficient, messed up search engines, and solve that challenge. Most of these search engines don't exist anymore.

The company could have failed if it had not started to consider their customer's emotions. Google continued to innovate and stick to its goal. Google concentrated on improving its algorithm every year, always a step ahead of their competitors. After all, consumers are dedicated only to their feelings. If another search engine emerged that was faster and more accurate, then Google Search would have been a thing of the past. Google continued to work on its superiority in search and will continue to do so. The google team did not mess up with the Google Search with extra features. It does the work we customers want it to do.

A few years after its initial success, Google made money without frustrating its customers, maintaining its excellent services free. Businesses that wanted to market their services to web surfers were paying Google's expenses. They still are. It is the business that expects to pay extra to generate sales, so businesses are happy customers too. It is a great model where everyone wins.

However, in most cases, entrepreneurs don't get it right. We can easily get confused by our emotional needs. While creating a new product, a team can lose track of the important principle of sales: reducing frustration or giving joy to an emotionally driven customer. As creative persons, we project our ideas and desires into the product, thinking "If I like this, our customers will too." What a load of crap!

We are not creating a product for ourselves. The emotions of the audience are always different from us. The same as the CD example, we might be movie streamers while attempting to sell to CD collectors. Completely different motivations.

In general, if we lose concentration and start to do what we feel is right to our taste, the product will, for sure fail in the market. If you have ever heard of "feature creep" in product design, then you understand what I mean. For those who don't, "feature creep" is the idea of everyone on the team adding great features to a product they think would make the product great. After some time, the product's main function, and the solution gets lost in a jumble of features the clients never asked for. As investors and entrepreneurs, we must keep our eye on the prize. If we apply the problem in the market, just like Google Search did, we'll be okay.

Another example of thinking of taking the wrong way is the 2013 attempt by Burger King to serve healthier food for a population that was more health-conscious. So they thought of "Satisfries," a reduced-calorie French fry. The challenge was, the food people at Burger King forgot their clientele never wanted a healthier French fry. If they wanted something healthy, they could go for the salad that was already on the menu or visit a restaurant offering healthier food. This time Burger King did not realize that few people went to their restaurant to purchase healthier fries. They loved their fries greasy and salty. Therefore, the final product flopped, and Burger King removed the Satisfries from menus after some months.

Sometimes, designers of product and entrepreneurs forget purchases are emotional altogether. Solving frustration via invention or design takes guts because it is risky. Some companies can beat us to the punch, we can misread the customer's emotional needs, and many other things could go wrong. Usually, companies forget the golden rule and duplicate an existing product in the market, hoping that the product will sell. This works if it focuses on a demographic not directly served by the main innovator. In case the product sells to a different audience, it means we have solved the issued for another type of person. The design could be similar, but a separate group of people is buying the product.

So, when considering a new product, no additional features and distractions. Maintain the solution clean with a clear message of how it fixes an emotional desire. An old marketing narrative says it all. "To develop a wooden deck, we don't go to the hardware store to buy drill bits; we visit the hardware store to identify a tool to drill holes."

The critical point of the story is that the solution may be drill bits, but if the creator finds a better, cheaper way to build holes, he or she will purchase that. That's the thinking that results in products that sell, and hence successful businesses.

We are walking talking balls of emotions. Our customers are similar. They won't reason with you. They only want solutions to feel more comfortable in whatever they are doing. Solve that basic emotional need and customers will purchase your product. Simple as that.

Why Emotions Are Important in Business

Emotions drive every element of our daily lives. They play a role in virtually every decision we make, whether it is connected to the business or our private lives.

Even decisions that are formulaic or methodical such as completing a tax return-will to some extent, be motivated by emotions.

Although emotions may at first look like abstract notions, it is possible to study and measure them with accuracy.

Emotions in business are critical. If you are more emotionally connected to your computer than people, maybe this is not for you.

As a consumer, what drives you to purchase a product from company A instead of B?

Is it because company A product is superior to that of company B? Maybe company A delivers it to your doorstep faster?

Or is it because of a less tangible reason-maybe you like the company's message, such as its decision to contribute 1% of its top line revenues to those in underserved communities?

It the modern hyper-competitive landscape, it seems complicated for companies to differentiate themselves from the crowd.

The main point is that people are making a purchasing decision depending on the emotion. As entrepreneurs and investors, we see this happen all the time. We argue that emotions drive most purchasing decisions these days.

You might have realized a trend in companies engaging your emotions. Why are they doing this?

Put. People don't purchase your product. They buy your story. And these stories should have an emotional win. People want to feel good about the product that they buy. Gone are the days when having a superior product gives companies a competitive advantage. Customers often expect an extremely high level of service, and that is why you need to differentiate by utilizing emotions.

You may think that the answer is obvious. The mission of your company must tell a story that attracts customers. If customers see your company's dedication to fair labor standards, they will be much ready to engage with your brand.

You are right but are likely missing an even critical consideration. The mission of your company must tell a story that attracts your employees.

What is less clear, but very important is the effect that your emotional appeal has on your workplace culture.

We have seen a significant share of different company cultures—the bad, the good, and the ugly—and we can testify the need of a story that resonates with your employees.

When they are on-board with the mission, they will strive to convince the customers to join as well.

Having a clear story and mission that attracts both your customers and your employees will help you stand out. The customers will consider your mission more than just a statement, and this can be your competitive advantage. If your employees are emotionally invested and your culture integrates your story, then your company is fore sure transparent.

On the other hand, if your story is disingenuous, and it is clear that your employees don't have a vested interest in the company's mission, customers see the actual colors. And that will lead to them not purchasing your product.

If customers don't see what your company is preaching, they will move on. With fewer methods for companies to differentiate themselves from their competitors, you must learn to stand out. And one of the best ways to stand out is to create a brand that taps into customer emotions.

When you allow emotions to get the best of your business, it is good for business and helps to gain loyalty while setting yourself the head of the pack.

Here are four main reasons why emotions in business are valuable

1. Emotions are a leading indicator
2. Emotions drive business: if you have ever started your own business or brand, then you know what this means. We become emotionally invested because our ideas are our creation. The passion we build with, and the drive it takes to launch a new approach is exciting. That excitement is the driver for our engine.
3. Emotions make us different than machines: If leadership was adhering to a series of events or instructions for the desired result, how would we progress? We would have done the same things,

the same way every day like machines. To request people to eliminate emotions would be to remove creativity and reasoning. When we question the status quo, it is to develop a result that is different and hopefully improved. Challenging the status quo is saying you aren't satisfied, so let's build a better outcome. Machines don't care about the result.
4. Emotions are what improves our connection: Our connection to our work is not just about the work itself. It is about the people we spend most of our time with. That connection builds from years of seeing each other through emotional highs and lows — deaths, wins, births, excitement, etc. We are connected through emotions. Emotions are the foundation of our relationships, and the relationships are the bedrock of business.

How do emotions affect decision making?

When you have a big decision to make, do you rely on your gut feeling, or do you create a list of pros and cons?

Following your intuition can be an excellent way to tune in to your genuine desires. But even when you think your decisions depend on logic, and common sense, they are always driven by emotion.

By understanding how emotions affect our decision-making process, we can learn to find the right balance between reason, and intuition, to create choices that serve us in living our best life.

How are decisions driven by emotion?

Emotions are build when the brain interprets what is happening around us through our memories, beliefs, and thoughts. This triggers the way we feel and behave. All our decisions are affected by this process in some way.

For instance, if you are feeling happy, you could decide to walk home using a sunny park. But if you had been chased by a dog as a child, that same sunny park might activate feelings of fear, and you would board a bus instead. There might be logical arguments to be made; either way, the decision is driven by your emotional state.

Emotions affect the decision in different forms. For instance, if you are sad, you might be willing to agree to things that you do not prefer. Still, sadness can make you generous.

Not only can emotions affect the nature of the decision, but the speed at which you decide. Anger can result in impatience and quick decision-making. If you are happy, you might make a quick decision without factoring the effects. Although if you feel afraid, your choices could be clouded by uncertainty and caution, and it might take you longer to select.

What this implies is that your gut feeling plays a big part in our decision-making process, but sometimes it can steer you wrong. It can lead to poor judgment, recklessness, and unconscious bias. But are there ever events when we need to pay attention to our gut feelings?

Should we always ignore the intuition?

A visceral response to a particular situation can be a survival means. The flash of fear experienced by early humans who encountered a dangerous animal motivated them to RUN NOW! They would not have survived if they stopped to think.

Alternatively, if you experience a terrible feeling in the pit of your stomach because of a specific situation, it could be your body's means of telling you it senses danger, depending on your past beliefs and experiences.

This reaction might be completely unfounded, but it can also serve to save you from danger or prevent you from repeating past mistakes.

This reveals one of the huge benefits of instinctive decision making-it is quick. If you are in a life, or death instance, you don't want to waste time dealing with the pros and cons.

This is true at the other end of the spectrum, too, when faced with a decision about something completely insignificant. No one should spend hours thinking about the relative advantage of tea over coffee.

Emotions vs logic

When handling people, keep in mind that you are not interacting with creatures of logic, but with creatures of emotion, animals that are driven by pride and vanity.

What is the correct way to use our minds? What is the most important? The head or the heart? Logic or emotions? The supporting arguments on both philosophy and emotions are so strong. Which side would you select?

Even though I like to follow these emotions-versus-logic debates closely, I highly support using our reasoning and thinking alongside all of the capacities of our mind. That is the reason why I believe the more we understand how our brain works, the better able we are to use it to change our lives.

When it comes to this duality, it is not in favor of one or the other, but it all about the right application of both. The reality is that we need both emotions and logic for practical problem-solving. To truly use our minds in the right way, we must involve the gut-check factor plus the thinking.

No matter where we feel them, both logic and emotions, are created within the brain.

The rational part of our brain is found in the frontal lobes, while the emotions develop from within the limbic system deep within our brain. Some of us could be tempted to think that emotions arise from our heart. This is the reason why we actively part our chest to say "I feel it right here."

The reason for this connection is that emotions develop with physical sensations. These sensations are always strong enough to speed our heart rate, change how we breathe, and even make the body temperature rise or drop. This is a rapid mechanism by which the brain alerts us to intense emotions and signals that we need to pay attention.

The logical parts of our brain are taking on the hardest part of collecting data, analyzing and sorting through all the information present. They perform the pros and cons analysis, correct for biases, estimate damages and costs, and lastly propose solutions. However, it is not wise to act on these proposals right away without confirming with our feelings.

The gut-check step is responsible for the approval of our last actions. Regardless of how logical a solution sounds, we always wonder whether it feels right. What is intuition saying to us? If you think about it, this will make sense:

Emotions are basically where all the problem-solving always starts and also where it stops.

When something feels dreadful and scary, these emotions alert the brain to do the work of analysis and evaluation, so that we can decide what to do concerning our feelings.

Once that process is done, it is the feelings that will direct us, once again as to which kind of solution feels okay and which one to follow. That is the perfect way to apply our mind: from feelings to logic, and back to the feelings again.

The easiest way to look at it is to see the kind as the result of the work that logic and emotions do together.

Our brain will take in mental energy in equal measure to process emotions, as it does to process any other type of information. This should be sensible if we understand that-for the brain-emotions are only another type of information. If you were to select, my guess is, you would perhaps want to spend additional time thinking and processing thoughts around your goals and the work you are doing. Most likely, you would rather not work with emotions, because they can be unclear, leaving us confused as to what to do about them.

We don't have this option, however. Emotions always come up as part of our normal functioning and as reactions to the world. What we need to do is to learn to handle them.

When we are well armed with the skills of "reading" and "decoding" our emotions, our knowledge of their meaning improves dramatically. With practice, we develop the kind of emotional fluency that allows us to process them quicker and more efficiently. If we consider emotions as a problematic puzzle, they will tend to overwhelm us. When we are caught up in them, we need to apply a lot of energy to determine what we are dealing with.

Simple tools of the mind enable us to remain balanced when processing different kinds of information, including emotions.

The most critical tool of the mind questions. Don't forget to ask: "Is there more to this?" What else do I need to know? What does this imply?" These questions make us consider all that is necessary, before jumping to conclusions. The third question is the most significant when we are handling emotions.

We are likely to react defensively. For that reason, we are also expected to overestimate the importance of what is happening. So, asking the correct questions helps us to put things into perspective.

Striking the correct balance for this collaboration between analytical thinking and emotions is the role of self-awareness.

This work usually requires years of practice. It is exciting and powerful work and brings a sense of peace and happiness to our lives.

The problems don't disappear, of course, but they do feel less like heavy burdens. When we learn to integrate emotions with reasoning, we are on our way to building resilience. Although it takes years to become a pro in self-awareness and attain this balanced form of thinking, the practice can start at any time. And it begins with the simple set of questions. This practice provides us with a realistic perspective on what is happening.

We have to remain objective because the easiest person to deceive is ourselves.

We might want to tell ourselves a different story about what is essential and what we are feeling. This can happen both ways. We might overestimate our strength or make light of the situation. We might also be absorbed by the drama of life, always self-inflicted, while doing very little of our work.

As a result, we must frequent but short internal check-ins. These check-ins can allow us to recover the integration of logic with emotions. We can ask ourselves:

- Are we lost and struggling with feelings?
- Are we overthinking?
- Maybe, on the contrary, we can act impulsively. What is the outcome of our action?
- How is our thinking-feeling balance?

These check-ins are some of the tips towards realizing a balanced integration. Such a balanced approach involves emotions and reasoning. This union of the mind is what develops a sense of well-being and, resilience in the face of adversity.

The Role of Emotions in Decision Making

Everyone would agree that emotion plays a critical role in marketing, but what isn't recognized is generating engagement and decision making.

The modern consumers are filled with a lot of marketing comms, and unsurprisingly, only a minuscule of that succeeds. Averagely, we are exposed to around 5, 000+ brand messages every day, but we only know about 86 with 12 achieving a lasting impression.

Therefore, the percentage we engage with is small and the rate that has any effect on us is even lower, although marketers expect a significant amount of cognitive reflection to be used to consuming their brand messages. This isn't sensible.

Human beings don't have the time to process the amount of information reflectively; instead, we apply subconscious signals in the form of feelings and thoughts that are defined by emotion, to make us remain attentive. Passion works as a cueing system.

Emotion command a significant action potential and can allow consumers to receive messages they would not accurately perceive in another way, so if brands want to limit the noise and optimize messaging to drive action, they have to consider the power of emotion.

Contrary to what is believed, all decisions are informed by emotion. A new study into the brain's action pathways has helped us understand the way emotion translates results into action. We apply emotions both as an appraisal tool and a guide for behavior.

In the past, an important role in a consumer's attention to marketing was to acquire information about a product.

In the Information Age, this is no longer a significant need. Marketing has to seek to drive consumer action, not through information but through an emotional connection to realize these modern primary needs.

So a brand that appreciates how human behaviour is driven by subconscious signals in the form of emotions can optimize their marketing. But like people, brands always go wrong by believing some universal emotions and myths.

There are two kinds of emotions, negative and positive, and these emotions have significant effects on our health and decisions. Research indicates, and even scientist understand that positive thoughts, feelings, and mindset have a healing state on the body.

Every small and big disease and illness is healed through a positive mindset, emotions, and feelings. An individual positive mindset can affect immunity rate at which a person can recover from illness and injury. Not only do negative emotions affect our health but also our feelings. We are emotional beings, and most of the time, we don't make decisions logically but emotionally, and thus, decisions made emotionally can destroy our lives and also interfere with our choices.

1. Over-excitement

This emotion can force you to make wrong decisions; the odds of getting over-excited occur when you are feeling happy.

For instance, at the time of festivals, people tend to become emotionally charged, and hence, they do not think a lot about money, and they are ready to pay even more.

2. Sadness

Research indicates that when you are under the influence of negative emotions, we tend to set low goals, we begin to keep low expectations from ourselves and this little expectation will finally restrict us from realizing our greatest potential.

Emotions play a significant role in decision making, so you need to understand your feelings, know your feelings, and master how your feelings and emotions affect you. Once you know it, you will know how to control it.

Ways emotion can screw up your decision making

Have you ever thought of some of the terrible decisions you have made, and asked yourself what was in thinking? Well, there is a chance you were not thinking. Instead, you might have acted on emotion, not logic.

Whether you dated a handsome man who maltreated you, or you wasted a lot of money on a terrible investment, your feelings can divert your attention if you are not careful. The stronger your emotions, the more your judgment might get clouded.

The correct decisions are taken when there's a balance between logic and emotions. When emotions are high, your thesis will be low, which can lead to irrational decisions.

Here are four ways your emotions can affect your judgment

1. **Excitement can make you overestimate your probability of success**

Casinos use bright lights as a means to make you feel excited. The happier you feel, the more likely you will want to spend money.

The moment you are excited about something; the chances are that you might not consider the risk. Whether you are requesting a big loan or you are placing all your cash on an impressive horse, you are likely to forget all the risk.

2. Anxiety is one part of your life spreads to other areas

If you are feeling anxious about something happening in your personal life maybe you are worried about a health scare, or you are nervous about purchasing a new home, it can make you feel anxious over your business decisions. Although the situation is entirely unrelated, research shows that you have a high probability to separate the two.

When you feel nervous, you might refuse to create change, or you could struggle to make decisions. Therefore, your thinking is likely to be clouded.

3. Anger and embarrassment can make you take a long shot

Strong emotions can result in rapid decisions if you aren't careful. Rage and humiliation can make you vulnerable to high-risk, low pay-off choices. Researchers believe string uncomfortable emotions affect self-regulation skills.

4. Sadness can make you settle for low

Studies show that you are likely to set low goals when you are feeling sad. Setting low expectations for yourself can prevent you from realizing your highest potential.

Balance emotion and logic

Emotions play a massive role in the decision making the process. Anxiety can prevent you from making a poor decision, whereas boredom can trigger a spark that makes you follow your passion.

To create balanced choices, understand your emotions. Pay attention to your feelings and understand how those emotions might interfere with your thinking and influence your behaviour.

Increase your logic and reduce your emotional reactivity by outlining the pros and cons of a complicated decision. By looking at the facts on paper, can allow you to reason about your considerations and limit your emotions from getting the best of you.

Emotional Intelligence at The Workplace

Emotional intelligence is the ability of a person to manage and control his or her emotions. It is a vital ability, especially in interpersonal communication.

Understanding the meaning of emotional intelligence and why it is critical in the workplace is very important. By nature, human beings are emotional creatures, but only emotionally intelligent can understand emotions. Both their own and others-and work with them to realize the best possible result for everyone. Within the framework of emotional intelligence, you will see opportunities to succeed personally and professionally.

Listing examples of emotional intelligence at the workplace

The importance of emotional intelligence at work are many, and the organization can utilize the power of emotional intelligence to set themselves apart from their competitors.

Prioritize emotional intelligence

Apart from what employees from other generations might have believed, people cannot turn off their emotions when they head to work –nor should they!

The focus for business leaders is to shed away preconceived notions concerning what a boo meant to do and approach a situation with a mind of emotional intelligence. Knocking your feet and shouting at your employees to work harder might result in improved short-term work results, but the long term effect will probably be disastrous.

These days, employees don't require their boss to become their best friend, but they want a relationship of respect and trust. If they fail to get it, they will look for a manager who provides it to them.

On the other hand, leaders who apply emotional intelligence at work to boos relationships will realize that their employees are more loyal and work better. Don't forget that emotional intelligence is connected to better physical health and mental health.

Having this in mind, employers should aim to hire and upgrade people who demonstrate signs of emotional intelligence, and they should strive to increase the emotional intelligence of their current employees.

A word of caution: research indicates that an individual with more emotional intelligence is not necessarily going to be useful. This means, when you take into consideration another person qualifications for a given role, emotional intelligence is just one of the many factors.

Build a culture that supports emotional intelligence

Like any skill, EQ requires practice. For that reason, organizations should develop a culture where employees and managers can practice and perfect their EQ.

The first step is to demonstrate to your employers that your organization cares. Remember, individual success results in organizational success.

However, what about emotional wellbeing? Do your employees know that you care about them as individuals? Once they do, they will be willing to follow you.

When you get support on an emotional level, remain at that level. If you switch to giving instructions after appealing to employee emotions, then the emotional work that you have invested will show up as being manipulative. A real emotional intelligence requires genuineness, and a genuine instance of emotional intelligence is more inspiring than words alone.

Define goals to boost emotional intelligence

Once you finish helping your employees realize their vision, try to boost emotional intelligence among your workforce.

Emphasize the need for actions like empathetic communication and set goals at every stage that can be linked to pillars of emotional intelligence.

Why EQ is important in the workplace

1. Work success depends on human interaction

While most workforces involve a different blend of skills and competencies, how they work together to realize their mission goal is the result of their ability as humans to collaborate.

This always shows up in soft critical skills like teamwork and communication. For instance, the partnership is about connecting to and understanding others, plus knowing how to create and maintain meaningful relationships. It also involves the ability to self-manage and motivates to effectively contribute to a big picture.

Emotional intelligence is the basis of all these skills and traits. It is bearing on the minutest of workplace interactions.

2. It is a vital element of leadership

As a leader, you are responsible for various financial and material resources. Your most crucial commodity will probably be your people, and the way you control them can make or break both your success and theirs.

At the center, people management is the ability to reveal and implement keen emotional awareness regularly.

Learning what makes people work, and how to use that to benefit the team, is an essential role of EQ. Most important, empathy is a critical leadership quality, that when used well, can ensure the loyalty of a team. By learning how people think and feel, it is easier to make better decisions, and you will be more rounded and respected as a leader.

It is not just how you get the best out of others, either. By understanding your limits, and your ability, it can be easier to control and manage your workload, making sure that you keep stress to a controllable level and remain active as a boss.

3. It is clear by its absence

All the ugly elements of a toxic workplace, such as discrimination are because of poor emotional intelligence. A failure of senior members and colleagues to empathize and understand on a basic human level is an excellent sign that an organization will not be productive, and subsequently not be successful. In this case, a toxic culture is built, and it becomes hard to eliminate.

Even the inability of persons to work together can cause trouble. Therefore, it is not a surprise that in recent years, a lot of organizations have tried to handle this issue at source by coming up with evident company culture.

4. It is a great recruitment tool

For HR managers, emotional intelligence is of excellent quality. This is the reason why applicants are carefully examined to find out how they can align with the culture of the organization.

Employers now want individuals who can demonstrate emotional intelligence in their responses. This provides the recruitment team with a sense of direction and goes along to ensure firms, whether big or small only hire the right people.

5. It is important for career success

If you had not realized, emotional intelligence is important in virtually every element of our working life. It is the reference for building relationships with coworkers, understanding weaknesses and motivations, and keeping ourselves in the right working state. In other words, without it, we cannot get very far in our careers.

Whether that success comes in the form of earning a promotion, creating a successful business, or landing a dream job, it doesn't matter. The ability to understand human nature is often going to be vital to arriving at your goal.

While there is a lot of ingredients in success, emotional intelligence is one of the most critical. You can study numerous degrees, have many years of experience and be as excellent at your job as it is humanly possible to be, yet if you don't understand people, you will never be successful in any element of your life.

So, continue to concentrate on building your social and emotional awareness, and remain conscious of how important it is to both yourself and the working environment around you. After all, it is your career that will fully benefit, plus the careers of those around you.

Chapter 2: EQ Models Every Business Leader Need to Know

Most people think that the characteristics that make a great leader are traditional traits such as drive, charisma, and vision. But what is more critical than all the other features and is present in all of the best leaders is emotional intelligence. The best leaders are said to be emotionally intelligent; this means they can understand their own emotions and those of others.

1. Self-Awareness

When you are self-aware, you understand your own emotions and how it affects your level of performance. You know why you are feeling and how it impacts what you want to achieve. You think how others look at you, and your self-image demonstrates that big reality.

You earn a sense of your strengths and limitations, which creates a realistic self-confidence. It further delivers clarity on your knowledge of purpose, so you become decisive when you set a course of action.

Self-aware leaders understand when their emotions hurt their work, or on the people close to them. They are then better positioned to address it in an effective manner, such as through building opportunities for feedback, experimenting with various ways to boost their team, or becoming open to creative solutions.

Self-awareness is one of the rubrics of a great leader. It demonstrates the ability to examine your actions, beliefs, and that of others. But not many people lack this ability.

Rarely, we set aside time to reflect on the truth and our thoughts.

The thoughts, beliefs, and perceptions we experience create the world around us. There is no argument to that. You understand the things you see around you; certain things are facts. But try to consider it for a moment from a different angle.

Psychology shows that our fundamental beliefs in life are nurtured before we reach the age of five. Without a great deal of conscious work, they change a bit throughout our lives. A lot of what we learn and experience from this viewpoint is filled with these beliefs.

Well, how does this connect with object reality

Well, this means that reality is experienced in different forms by each person. Every experience you have had, the beliefs that you have created, the opinions you have, affect how you experience the current truth. The same way no two people can have similar experiences throughout life; everyone goes through a different reality in any given moment. So, there is no objective reality, just that which is developed by the mind.

Why self-awareness is critical for leaders

Self-awareness is the most reliable indicator of success. Being aware of one's weaknesses allows executives to work with others who have different abilities, they can accept the idea that a different person might have better skills than their own, and thus benefit from that. A lack of self-awareness can separate others, through misunderstanding the effect of your actions on them.

It is a difficult skill to define. Most people consider themselves as being self-aware when they aren't. It is highlighted by psychologists that those who claim to understand themselves the best are always the least self-aware.

Self-awareness is a continuous process.

It is not something that you acquire by a one-off personality assessment that defines you as fitting into a box or as a series of letters.

It is a process of reflection that happens over the years.

It is a continuous checking back in with the self to determine where you are at. How others see you and what your current strengths and weaknesses are.

It is trying to change and understand where you are at and how your thinking and actions are affected by your experiences. Where do your biases stand, and how can you overcome these so that the world can be seen more realistically?

Developing self-awareness

Awareness of your emotions and self can be developed. Just spend time to identify areas that you need to improve and make an effort to strengthen that part of your life.

You can become more aware of your strengths and areas you need to develop by:
- Rate yourself
- Fill a formal assessment test

- Request others for feedback

Emotionally intelligent people plan to set aside some time to improve their awareness. One way you can achieve this is by reflecting daily.

This means that you create a silent place for yourself in the day, other activities, and spend time concentrating on doing something that opens your mind to more profound thoughts.

Values, assumptions, and beliefs

Standards, ethics, and principles control our lives. Understanding your values is an integral part of improving awareness of yourself.

Understanding your values is like following a well sign-posted road. You are secure because you know where you are, you know where you are going, and you are confident, as well as happy understanding that you are on the perfect road.

Assumptions

Becoming aware of the assumptions we hold about others is a vital element of emotional intelligence. Assumptions we carry can be negative or positive. Negative assumptions consist of thoughts such as "It is only me that bad things happen" or "I don't have enough information to start my business."

The beliefs that we hold about ourselves are critical because they predict our behavior.

To develop a massive self-awareness of knowledge means to have a clear grasp of reality.

Self-awareness is a vital element of emotional intelligence. Being self-aware is a process, and you will probably spend time learning about yourself. But as you increase your level of self-awareness, you also improve your experience of life, develop opportunities for better work-life balance.

Self-control

Understanding your emotions and their impact is one thing, but a critical aspect of emotional intelligence is self-control. This is the ability to refocus negative emotions into constructive action. For instance, fear does not fail to act but encourages the leader to deal with the thing they fear.

Self-control can be described as personal accountability or remaining in control of your emotions. If you are tempted to direct your frustrations on someone else, instead of holding your breath, try to write down the negative comments on a paper, and shredding it. This can be helpful for releasing steam and staying calm.

Self-control, or discipline, is a critical element that every leader with crucial responsibilities must-have. However, restraint is rarely visible on any list of the important traits that make a great leader. Passion, confidence, clarity, communication, and empathy all appear on these lists, but not self-control.

Requirements of leadership qualities focus on the behaviour and results instead of character or fundamental psychological abilities.

While the corporate world tends to underestimate self-control, professional investors value it. Seasoned investors are aware that they are prone to mistakes in judgment when emotion overrides rational decision making. They also are aware that this can and will happen to all of them. They remain alert and search for means to prevent emotion-driven mistakes, including "jumping on the bandwagon," responding out of fear or excessive caution or being influenced by envy and greedy.

A leader who demonstrates strength in the area of self-control shows composure and confidence, remaining task-focused in a depressing situation.

Great leaders exercise self-control. Demonstrating self-control requires one to manage their emotions and impulses to eliminate inappropriate reactions and disperse energy in a positive way.

Self-control allows good leaders to remain calm and clear-headed at the time of a crisis, or at a time of high stress. A self-controlled leader will also act strategically rather than react. When you have self-control, you can avoid short-term gain and wait for a huge payout.

What does a lack of control in a leader feel like? Getting angry is a common reaction. Instead of exercising leadership, some will act like a two-year-old child who throws a public temper tantrum. This behaviour generates stress in an organization, a loss of team productivity, and makes a leader lose influence over others.

Others become irritable and impatient. The signs of impatience and irritability comprise of interrupting others, a lack of listening and put-downs. This negative tendency can become contagious in a company.

Lastly, a lack of control can make a leader act on impulse. If not checked, it can result in excessive greed and addiction and probably a moral failure.

How to boost self-control

- **Realization-**Reflect the actual value of whatever is tempting you. Once you devalue your temptations, understand the results of acting, and see the amount of longer-term goals, you are likely to align yourself towards those goals and avoid any temptation.

- **Pre-commitment:** Make critical decisions before you get into a tempting situation. Setting targets for yourself can help you move on when you are about to give up. Additionally, understanding your walk-away is crucial to avoid regretting during a negotiation. The point is to eliminate the number of options you have in the future.
- **Avoidance:** Understand the times when your self-control is low and avoid the temptation during those times.

Ten ways to master self-control

The biggest obstacle in life sits within ourselves. For that reason, you must be self-discipline.
Like everything else that builds progress, the greatest struggle is always within ourselves.

Individuals with a higher level of self-control have minimal time to decide whether to take part in actions that are dangerous to their health. They don't let impulses or feelings guide their choices.

However, they create level-headed decisions. As a result, they feel satisfied with their lives.

Check out these ten ways to master self-discipline.

1. Remove temptations

By getting rid of the biggest temptations from your surroundings, you will highly increase your self-discipline.

If you want to take a healthy diet, you have to avoid junk food. If you're going to become more productive at work, turn off notifications and keep your phone on silent mode. The fewer distractions you have, the more focused you will be on achieving your goals. Prepare yourself for success by eliminating bad influences.

2. Grow your self-discipline

We are not born with self-control; it is a learned behaviour. Similar to any other skill you want to master, it demands daily practice and repetition. Willpower and self-discipline require a lot of work. The effort and focus that self-discipline demands can be draining.

As time elapses, it can be more challenging to maintain your willpower. The bigger the temptation, the more challenging it can feel to handle other tasks that demand self-control. So strive on improving your self-discipline through constant diligence.

3. Set clear targets and create an implementation plan

If you want to become self-discipline, you need to develop a clear vision of what you hope to become. You must also have some knowledge of what success means to you. If you don't know where you are heading, it is easy to lose your way, or even get sidetracked.

A clear plan shows every step you must take to attain your goals. Determine who you are and what you care about. Develop a mantra to remain focused. Successful people apply this approach to stay on track and develop a solid finish line.

4. Reward yourself

Reward yourself something to be proud of what you have achieved. You can set goals, and once you reach a goal, reward yourself with a present. When you know that you have something waiting for your once you hit a given target, it makes you concentrate on accomplishing that goal after you achieve your goal. Set a new purpose.

5. Forgive yourself and move forward

Even when you think you have done everything to achieve whatever you want. You will experience challenges which may slow you down. Don't give up, but keep moving forward. If you are knocked down, acknowledge the root cause and keep going. Don't be trapped in guilt or anger, and these emotions will only block your way and impact your progress. Learn from your mistakes and learn to forgive yourself.

6. Understand your weaknesses

Nobody is perfect. And so, we will keep making mistakes, but how you react once you make a mistake is essential. Understand your weaknesses and find ways to overcome them. Most people try to assume like they have no flaws, but that is not true. If you acknowledge your fault and take the necessary steps to avoid them, you will be okay.

7. Change your perception about willpower

A research conducted by Stanford University discovered that your amount of willpower is defined by your beliefs. This means if you believe your willpower is less, then you won't surpass the limits. However, if you don't set a target on your self-control, you are likely to get tired before you achieve your goals.

Keep in mind that your internal belief about self-control and willpower determines how much you have. If you can filter out these mental obstacles and believe that you can do it, then you will gain double strength and motivation to realize those goals.

8. Create a backup plan

Psychologists designed a technique to increase willpower. This technique was named "implementation intention." In this technique, you are supposed to come up with a plan to handle the potential severe problems you may face. For instance, say you want to eat a healthy diet, so you set rules that will forbid you from consuming junk food, then one day your close friend invites you to attend a birthday party where junk food is going to be served.

If you apply this technique, you will need to say to yourself that you aren't going to take any plate of cheese and crackers, you will receive a glass of water and focus on interaction. Well, this might sound difficult to do, especially in a party, but that is what the "implementation intention" requires. However, if you think you might not handle the temptation of food at the party, you can also choose to turn down the invitation.

9. Create fresh habits and keep it simple

Being self-discipline and working hard to master a new routine can be tiresome. To prevent any frustrations, make the whole process simple. The best approach is to break down your goals into smaller steps. Now start to work on every more minor step. Don't try to complete an entire task at once, this will but intimidate you, and you will end up giving up.

If you are trying to get in shape, start by practising 10-15 minutes daily. If you want to create better sleep habits, aim to go to bed 15 minutes early. The point is to take small steps at a time.

10. Eat regularly

The feelings of being irritated, or angry when you are hungry are real. When hungry, it becomes difficult to concentrate, and your brain cannot function well. This means your work, self-control, and relationship are affected. To avoid these, ensure you eat healthy regularly. Your mind needs enough energy for it to work optimally.

Motivation

When we consider emotional intelligence, we understand that it is a complex problem that has internal and external factors that affect our emotions, behaviours, and thoughts. One of the significant aspects of emotional intelligence that sometimes is overlooked is self-motivation.

By definition, self-motivation refers to the ability to step out of bed every day, clean our homes, or go to work. It embodies our reasons for doing something. It is a mix of our drive, optimism, commitment, and persistence to do something beyond recognition.

While there are some people who are highly motivated, it doesn't mean that they can understand other components of emotional intelligence such as self-awareness. These people are not always driven to achieve things for reasons other than financial gain.

Where does motivation originate?

Motivating yourself and others to act begins with being open on what you want to accomplish. It doesn't have to be a critical, life-altering goal. Anything we look forward to, whether it's for a relationship, health, career, or adventure related purposes, it doesn't matter as long as we are open about what it means for us and those around us, and what we expect the result will be.

This way, we will concentrate on the benefits and outcome we expect, instead of the insecurities that are holding us back.

It is also critical to expect the constant setback and understand that any goals worth attaining are going to have effects along the way.

Commitment is important

A vital organ of motivation is remaining firm in our duties. When we make commitments to ourselves or others, and finally break them, we paint ourselves as unreliable and lack perseverance. While breaking a plan for a legitimately good reason is understandable, but being able to get back on our feet and resuming where we left off is what sets the difference. Breaking from commitments will diminish our ability to attain our goals and reduce our credibility and distance form our allies and supporters.

When we discuss motivation within the framework of emotional intelligence, we need to consider how we motivate others. Are we supportive, kind or optimistic, or we do apply bribery or even fear tactics? Being confident, having integrity, and sharing our optimism with others allow us to be great motivators. When speaking to our inner self that "I've got this, I can achieve this!" We always see good results. The same is true when we share positive energy with others. It is an excellent motivator. We can still remind others of the moments when they were super motivated and how amazing that all turned out. Cultivating dynamic behaviours and excellent communication skills helps us motivate others.

The saying, "' actions speak louder than words" is meaningful when it comes to inspiring others. Some of us can connect to that friend who always has lots of advice, but they are the opposite of a "poster child" for that topic.

How to improve your motivation?

You get to your work desk with every intention of starting your next project, then you procrastinate. Two hours later, you discover that you still haven't started the task. Why is it so easy to avoid doing something, even when you know the job must be done?

Research indicates that our minds are trained to have two kinds of motivation.

1. Internal motivation
2. External motivation

Internal motivation involves doing something that has a reward. On the other hand, external motivation consists of doing something so that you skip a punishment.

Every type of motivation is helpful. For long-term benefits, internal motivation is the best, but external motivation can be powerful in helping you finish a task that does not interest you.

The secret is to utilize both kinds of motivations to overcome procrastination to become proactive. Here are five brain hacks to enhance your motivation, and remain productive, even when distractions occur.

1. Don't overthink it

When you overthink, you make things difficult by expecting extraordinary challenges. When you overthink a task you are working on, it builds stress and pressure. Overall, it breaks your motivation.

Research indicates that chronic anxiety and stress can reduce your brain. A relaxed mind can focus on and solve issues that arise.

To overcome a tendency to overthink a problem, ensure that you keep your goals simple. This will break your objectives into manageable chunks. Concentrate on completing every step. This builds motivation because you see yourself moving forward and achieving your goals.

2. Enhance your greatest memories

If you boost your good memories, then you will also become inspired and motivated.

To achieve this, recall a time when you accomplished your goals. Imagine this memory as if it was being displayed on a big screen.

Make your memory bright and loud. Repeat this process 5-10 times, and you will remember that what was once a positive mind is now a great motivation. The more you experience the memory, the more you will want to make it real again.

3. Overcome mental obstacles

There is nothing terrible as a mental block that looks like a glued stack into your brain. Your creative process appears locked up, and nothing tends to work right.

Getting stuck is a sign you are caught in a negative thought cycle. To unstick yourself, start by reversing the thoughts. Take a deep breath, relax, and let your subconscious identify the answer.

4. Take advantage of your ultimate purpose

When you discover you lack motivation, try to concentrate on the meaning behind what you are doing or how it results in a broader goal of what you want to achieve.

5. Reverse negative perceptions

Pay attention to how you feel when you start a task. Are you worried about the assignment? Do you think it will be challenging to complete the job? This kind of mindset will deny you the motivation and inspiration.

However, you can change negative perceptions the same way you can wire your mind to avoid bad memories. To eliminate a pessimistic attitude, consider the task and bring the memory of doing it into your account.

Self-Motivation and how it will help you

You need to be 100% sure of the self-motivation definition if you want to achieve it.

Most self-motivation definitions you see out there miss the point. They focus on the ability to find the strength within yourself, without assistance from anyone. True, but where does that strength originate from?

The correct self-motivation is one where you are motivated by what you want. That might look like oversimplifying it, but it's not.

So, what is self-motivation

It's about what you truly seek. Many of us think we know what we want, but we don't. So we find ourselves motivated by the wrong things.

Check out this example. Some of the reasons you might want to go to a medical school include:

- I'm excellent at science: Wrong motivation.
- Doctors are paid well: Wrong motivation.
- My parents were both professional doctors: Even worse
- I love the way it feels to help people: The right motivation.

Well, what is the problem with the first three reasons? They are legitimate, and people make decisions based on that thinking daily.

Self-motivation vs. external motivation

Do you know the difference between self-motivation and external motivation?

According to Frances McIntosh of Forbes, external motivation appears in the form of a reward such as praise, money, and fame.

However, internal motivation is driven by our personal psychological needs. What this means is that we like to feel we are good at something, we are making a difference, and we love being self-directed as well as connected to others.

Most unhappy people are driven by day-to-day external motivations.

But if you are self-motivated, you will not go through your day to pay the rent; you are after something more significant. So the alarm goes off early in the morning and you're ready to go. You aren't dragged out of bed by an obvious thing. You want to wake up and chase that feeling.

Self-motivation and adversity

One of the signs that you know what you are after is that you don't allow anything to distract you from your main course. When you only see what you don't want, your intentions aren't focused. You are a bit shaky. But when you are focused, you respond well to adversity.

Let's assume you want to be a firefighter. You feel it is something you are capable of doing, and you would enjoy. Plus, the pay and benefits are handsome. A great career, for sure.

But then you realize the fees to be a firefighter is more than $20, 000. And suddenly becoming a firefighter gets big "no" and you decide that is not for you.

That is because your inspiration to become a firefighter had the best intentions, but was superficial. However, if being a firefighter was your dream and you had a burning desire to be, the cost would not have scared you.

You would have burned the midnight oil looking for scholarships or bursaries. Or you would have decided to seek for a loan, or do something to ensure money doesn't stop you from achieving your dream.

And in case another challenge came up, you will deal with it too.

How to remain self-motivated

Now that you understand the correct definition of being self-motivated, you can go after it. And that implies taking good care of yourself along the way.

Even when you are self-motivated, you aren't invincible. You need to take specific actions to ensure this fire never goes out and continues to burn as brightly as it is right now.

Here are some things that you can try out:

Reward yourself

Your reward should not just come at the finishing line. You need to reward yourself along the way for your great efforts. Not only is it a proven self-care approach, but it also changes the wiring of our brains to maintain motivation.

Elle Kaplan wrote a compelling piece at CNBC. He described a study that compared brains of motivated people to those who are lazy. The study found that dopamine levels in a given section of the brain played a significant role in people's ability to be self-motivated.

Kaplan wrote that dopamine is released in anticipation of a reward, and this means rewarding yourself for achieving something can help you stay on track.

You bet on yourself, and you win. You need to enjoy the winnings.

Hang out with the right people

When you hang out with people who are self-motivated, it makes you remain self-motivated. You should learn to share your wins and struggles with people who are driven by internal motivation. So look for a mentor or group of people. Their support and advice can move you forward.

Gerard Adams of Entrepreneur.com summed it well when he wrote that success doesn't happen from nothing, but there are several things that lead to success.

Hard work and drive are always needed to succeed as an entrepreneur, but your improvement leading to your success can highly be enhanced by others.

If your friends are motivated by external factors, they might not get it. Their complaints might not get much worse than, "yeah, work sucks." They will think you are abnormal to work as late as you do. However, self-motivated individuals will get it.

So you should always surround yourself with people who are still doing things, and not those who are always talking about doing things. The latter will often try something and give up along the way. But a self-motivated individual will keep going no matter what.

Keep learning

Read and try and to take everything you can. The more you learn, the more confident you are in starting projects.

Know yourself

Take note of when motivation sucks and when you feel like a superstar. You will see a pattern, once you know that, you can work around, and develop.

Up to now, you have learned more than an accurate definition of self-motivation. You have an understanding of what you need to do to become genuinely self-motivated and how to go after your goals.

The last word on motivation

We all try to make the most out of our lives, and it is normal for us to experience various levels of motivation, depending on our current state. It would be tedious if every part of our energy were concentrated on being highly motivated in all sectors of life. We need to stop and figure out why we are working towards a goal, and whom does it benefit? We also need to be transparent and uphold integrity in all that we do and help others understand that as well. Take some time to revisit your personal views on motivation, and explore different things, both internal and external, that inspire you.

Empathy

Empathy is defined as the ability to understand the feelings of the other person, or, at least their emotional reactions to things. It centres on the ability to "walk a mile in someone else's shore's," although we might not have personally experienced what they are going through, we understand and expect the situation and recognize that there are feelings and emotions connected to it. This does not mean that we need to share those emotions with them; we only need to know where they are coming from. But before we can be empathetic, we must have a good sense of our self-awareness and develop insight into our emotions. This is how we improve ourselves and expand our mindsets by looking at things from a different perspective. Think of a close friend who might share some information about finding a dream job, or overcoming severe illness.

An emotionally intelligent individual would likely respond to them with enthusiasm and delight, even though they have not personally experienced those things. The same is true with sadness, lousy news a person might have; we understand that being empathetic is critical, even if we don't know all the right things to speak or do. It is vital to appreciate and respect the feelings of others, even when we disagree with them or their decisions. Another indicator of an emotionally intelligent person is knowing when not to make comments or statements that are cruel or judgmental. It would be a cold and lonely world if individuals always responded with "I don't care" to numerous events, happenings, and feelings we share.

It is a social enterprise

We are social creatures, and you cannot avoid it. Emotionally intelligent individuals are genuinely interested in others and apply social skills to create and manage relationships in our personal and professional lives. Unless we are lighthouse keepers, we need to socialize at our workplace. This does not mean you go to hang out every day with friends or ask about everyone's lunch plans. What it means is that we need to be respectful and collaborative if we want to excel at work.

We must be sensitive to the diversity of different kinds. We grow and learn a lot from people who come from unique backgrounds than us, as we develop the chance to see things through a different lens. In the current multi-cultural society, we are lucky to meet so many new people with unique experiences to share.

Empathy and emotional intelligence in sales

Compassion is what makes a salesperson has a better knowledge of what their prospect is feeling. It is the patient understanding of the other person thoughts, emotions, and opinions. In part, it allows them to build a connection with their prospect and customers.

Emotional intelligence enhances that relationship. Although empathy causes the salesperson to understand what the potential customers are feeling, emotional intelligence is what makes them communicate that they understand their implications and feelings.

Altogether, these abilities allow the salesperson to understand the communication of the other person, including the hidden message in their words. Trying to understand the emotions, thoughts, and feelings of another person are the foundation of building trust.

You can spot these traits in great salespeople. You recognize it when their clients and prospects share their business challenges and opportunities with other salespeople. You see it in the way salespeople communicate, in a way that they understand the feelings of the customer.

Becoming a more empathetic leader

As a manager or business leader, there's a high chance that you spend most of the time building the skills and qualities that you believe will make you more productive at your job. These skills include vision, expertise, creativity, and decisiveness. While these are great traits for leaders to show, one of the most critical is empathy. This is what makes us human.

As said before, empathy is the ability to put yourself in the shoes of the other person and imagine how that individual feels. It is a great skill that people use in their daily lives as they interact with people around.

As numerous research show, empathy is crucial for leaders.

Managers who display increased levels of empathy toward their staff are considered as better performers by their employers.

But the most important is for leaders to interact with their members empathetically.

Why empathy is essential in business

There are so many theories that try to answer this question, but all of them point to the fact that we are all human beings.

The ability as a manager to understand the emotions that your team members feel not only makes you a great communicator but also creates rapport, trust, and connection that boosts team success.

Even more, empathy will not only guide your team, but it will allow you to request customers the questions that you must understand their goals, fears, objectives, and aspirations, which you can apply to improve your overall business plan and become profitable.

It is just challenging to overestimate the role of empathy in building a successful business.

Empathy makes employees work better with each other. Employees who are appreciated feel better and want to do more in their work, they want to do more for their fellow employees. When empathy is expressed at the top, it is channelled down throughout the whole company. This leads to more teamwork, less staff conflict, and low workplace interference. This partnership will lead to increased productivity and coordinated work effort.

One of the challenges that companies face is maintaining the talented staff. One of the most highlighted reasons for people leaving a company is the lack of trust and appreciation from those they report to. Empathy boosts confidence, a feeling that employees are appreciated, and taken care. Whether in personal relationships or as an organization, we are likely to stay when we feel like we are heard, cared about, and appreciated.

How to become a more emphatic manager or business leader?

If you want to become a better manager, then empathy is a skill that you can learn or improve upon.

Here are some things you can try to become a more empathetic leader

1. Be a great listener

The easiest ways to increase your empathy skills is to become a better listener. Keep in mind that every conversation you have is a chance to create relationships, create rapport, and support the free flow of ideas which can expand an innovative business.

Many people don't know how to listen. The good thing is that it is not hard to learn how to be a good listener. All you need to do is to pay attention, don't disrupt, or be distracted.

If you can follow those simple rules, you will become a good listener.

Of course, you don't just pay attention to the words that your team members are saying, but you also understand the emotions beneath those words, plus reading the nonverbal cues. Examples of nonverbal cues are a tone of voice, body language, gestures, etc.

Remember that communication is 80 per cent nonverbal, this means if you concentrate on the words being spoken, you will only be getting 20 percent of the message.

Besides making you an excellent communicator, practice your active listening skills to reveal to your team that you appreciate what they say, you value them, and their opinions.

2. Look at things from their perspective

There are moments when it is hard to understand the emotional state of your employees.

Maybe you have been assigned a new team of employees, and you have not had the time to build personal bonds. Or you might have joined a new organization where employees hide their genuine emotions from their leaders.

Whatever the cases, in such cases, there are still options that you can take to earn valuable emotional insight into the mindset of your employees.

One way that you can easily acquire some insight is to consider the point of view of your employees. If you were the one a similar situation, how would you feel? What would you have done? What would you expect from your manager? What would you not expect from your manager? Use these insights to create rapport and enhance the level of communication that you need to become effective at your job.

3. Build a personal connection with members of your team

Empathy involves reading and understanding the emotions experienced by others. One way that managers can become better at understanding is by putting in the work to create a bond with every team member.

Creating a more personal relationship helps you as a manager in various ways. First, it provides insight into the ways team members express their emotion. Remember, that no two people express feelings the same way, so taking some time to learn how every member you work with communicates is essential.

Besides this, a personal bond with your team members will help them see that you care about them and not just what they do. These bonds allow you to become friends with your team members, creating a culture of open communication that can result in innovative discussions and solutions to problems.

The power of empathy

The ability to empathize with your team is the most critical skill that any leader can show. Flexing your muscles for emotional intelligence will allow you to create a culture of open communication, understand the worries and motivations of your team, and build a relationship that will enable your organization to attain its strategic business goals.

Social Skills

Social skill is a broad term, but it is also used in the context of emotional intelligence. When it comes to emotional intelligence, the word 'social skills' describes the skills required to influence the emotions of others.

Great leaders need excellent social skills.

Social skills refer to the skills that you apply when you collaborate with others. They provide a way for interaction and boost productivity, increase your general quality of life, and improve relationships. People with this level of competency are easy to talk to, talented at resolving conflicts, excellent communicators, great team players, and skilled at building relationships.

Below are skills that account for skills and emotional intelligence.

Management of conflict

Those good at conflict management can recognize that conflict as a chance. It can help individuals or workgroup to:

- Improve processes
- Learn new skills
- Solve problems
- Heal rifts
- Boost relationships

Of course, resolving conflict demands a great deal of emotional intelligence. You must know how to identify the root cause of the conflict. For instance, a dispute involving how to phrase a new advertisement because one party feels like their input is not considered. In such a case, you need to understand the point of view of the people involved and make them reach an agreement. You need to know how you will handle communication in a productive style. Above all, you must seek for a win-win situation.

Teamwork and collaboration

This skill demands that you create a view of teams as individuals that need growth. For an organization to function, it has to be attended. An individual with emotional skill also knows that collaboration is an excellent tool for decision making, building relationship, and creating the perfect environment.

Individuals with this skill

- Share resources and information to enhance collaboration.
- Remember to concentrate on relationships and tasks.
- Search for opportunities to expand the abilities of the team.
- Look for methods for all members of the team to generate their strengths.

Creating bonds

Boosting emotional intelligence will improve your ability to develop relationships because your people skills, self-confidence, and communication skills will all be expanded. But if you concentrate on creating bonds, you will build a form of social network that will grow the number and type of relationships that you want to create.

Those with skill make efforts to:

- Work on building rapport
- Keep others informed
- Make friends at workplaces
- Spend time cultivating mutually beneficial relationships

If you gain this skill, you will begin to see relationships not just as things that 'happen,' but as bonds that you can proactively create. You will also develop a better relationship if you practice other emotional skills.

How social skills is changing leadership

There was a time when empathic skills were considered vulnerable skills that had no role in active management. However, for one to overcome the complex factors in successful leadership, leaders don't just need to be smart and ethical decision-makers, but they also need to demonstrate healthy social skills. They need to demonstrate social leadership.

Social leadership is appreciating that there is a team of individuals responsible for the development and implementation of all decisions and ideas. When speaking as a leader in terms of "I" has to be replaced with "We." However, becoming a social leader is more than just understanding there is a team; it is learning how to build trust, respect, and care within the team. These values will allow team members to share ideas and work together, generating an open atmosphere from which everyone has a lot of stake in guiding the company.

Mastering social leadership skills by building a relationship is very important if you want to become a great leader.

Becoming a social leader

Some people are born with excellent social skills, while others struggle to gain these skills. Regardless of whether leaders are born or not, social skills can be learned and acquired. For some, this could be difficult, but they are critical skills to have to guide a successful team. There are numerous features that natural social leaders have:

- Caring: They care about others and their overall being.
- Vulnerability: They are open and authentic with others.
- Resilience: They are balanced in the face of stress.
- Collaboration: They ensure that decisions are made as a team and have respect.
- Courage: They are able to do what is right, even though it cannot be easy.
- People and relationship-oriented: They understand that people and relationships are crucial to the health of the organization, and strive to enhance the social aspect of the company.

- Intuition: They can feel a situation and make decisions based on inner voice rather than reasoning.

If you are keen, you will realize that most of these traits point to a higher level of emotional intelligence, which result in quality management.

Well, **are you a social leader?**

These questions will help you tell whether you have the traits of a social leader, and if you are applying them in your leadership style:

- Do I try to think of means to avoid problems, instead of waiting for problems to happen before I switch into action?
- Do I prefer to listen to ideas from others when I am about to make decisions?
- Do I trust my employees to complete a task and do the correct thing?
- Do I let others see the real me when I interact with them?
- Do I give the group credit for ideas and positive results?
- Am I able to look at the bright side?

If you said yes to most or all these questions, then you already have traits of a social leader for items which you said no, try to figure out how that quality affects your employees.

If this is something you are interested in expanding, share these questions with your team, and find out what their responsibilities are. Inspire them to measure their social leadership ability.

Becoming a social leader

We are all social, and so everyone has features of becoming a social leader. However, in case the answers to these questions stated differently, there are specific things that can be done to make everyone a social leader.

One of the leading factors to being a social leader is the focus.

Focus is required to be in tune with the role and the work. Discussion leads to engagement. Interacting with the work and all elements of the work makes people apply their social skills to see how others are feeling, show empathy, and collaborate on a solution.

Focusing on the work and people can be a better way to deal with low morale, dissatisfaction, and burnout. Once a leader detects these things, they can respond quickly and take control of a situation, by getting in touch with people, and handling the case through communication.

In some situations, people need to be listened so that they feel they are being understood. This builds an atmosphere of worth and value. A social leader should listen and understand.

Leaders should not necessarily agree with employees, but they can listen and advice accordingly.

Research indicates that most people consider it necessary to work for a supportive boss than earn a lot of money. Leaders who take care of their employees boost their productivity.

Skills you must master as a social leader

1. Understand non-verbal cues

A great social leader doesn't depend only on one type of communication but is aware of written, verbal, non-verbal, and so on.

In today's world, it is challenging to read non-verbal cues because communication is digital. However, in face-to-face interaction, you must identify how your perception eliminates input.

2. Interact often

You don't necessarily need to know everyone, but you need to understand how customers, employees are thinking and reacting. This means you must interact with others proactively. You must be comfortable in-person to connect with employees on social channels. By reaching out to your employees early, you will gain valuable insights that you never expected.

3. Supports community presence

Social media is essential in the current world. Companies are on par with the current trends. As such, business reputation and results can be improved in online communities.

As a leader, you can support community presence through blogging on behalf of your company brand. Encourage members in your team to develop a virtual community.

4. Show genuine interest in your employees and others

You can fake some skills but you cannot fake sincerity. While some may consider this a personality attribute, not a skill. But sincerity is the difference between a leader and a task manager. If you aren't sincere, you will perform things that might make business sense, but finally, they will backfire.

5. Discuss your values and purpose

There are many reasons why people join companies, but why they choose to stay is because they feel appreciated, and a sense of purpose. It is important as a leader to stress on the mission, vision, use, and values of your company. That way, employees know where they are headed.

Self-awareness and Introspection

When you encounter challenges, where do you find the motivation to push forward? Many people get stuck from time to time, going through difficulties of life they know they could be better.

Knowing yourself better leads to a stronger relationship, a clear sense of purpose, and overall well-being. The benefits of self-awareness can be useful in almost every side of your life. They all make you a better person, parent, spouse, colleague, and friend.

How do you find answers to the problems you face?

Gaining a stronger self-awareness requires patience and time. You cannot learn it overnight. You have to do it time to time by coming up with a habit of self-reflection.

The next section will look at how you can apply introspection to discover life-changing insights.

If you want lasting change in life, then you need to practice self-reflection and introspection today.

The objective of self-awareness is the actionable insight you can apply to change your life for good. However, how can you access those insights? Self-awareness requires three aspects to get you where you want to reach:

- Self-Reflection-This involves contemplation, examination, and evaluation of one's feelings, thoughts, and actions.
- Introspection-This is the process of trying to directly access another person internal psychological processes, perceptions, judgments, and states.
- Insight-It is a clear and sudden discernment of a solution to a problem.

Introspection provides a chance for you to understand yourself, self-reflection makes you process what you learn, and insights are the responses you come up, and you can act upon.

Besides generating insights, self-awareness increases the chances that you will do as you say. Self-awareness increases your chances to exercise control over your emotions and decrease stress and anxiety.

Through self-awareness, you are less likely to veer off track when difficult emotions arise. Rather than doing something that you will later regret, you will be equipped to eliminate emotional troughs.

Introspection method: Do's and Don'ts

Don't become obsessed

You don't need to think about yourself all the time. That will not result in more in-depth knowledge. If you are not careful about how you reflect on your life, you could end up feeling sad than happy. Studies indicate that individuals who spend most of the time in introspection "tend to be more anxious, and more negative attitudes about themselves. And the reason is that they are doing it wrong.

Don't ask wrong questions

When you take part in introspection, you always start by asking questions; it could be as simple as, "Why do I feel this way?" You look for reasons beneath your discontent. On the surface, it is realistic, but it can result in misery. The reason is when you ask why, the brain switches to the most general answer. Usually, you pick one that verifies your pre-existing beliefs. That is because our significant motives are beyond our conscious awareness. It takes great effort to uncover the root causes. We resort to answers that feel right at the moment. However, these easy answers are often wrong.

For instance, if you lose your temper at a colleague, you could think, "I can't just work with her. She hurts me badly." But the main reason why you snapped might because you are anxious about a performance review that is about to be done.

That's why asking why questions are the wrong type of self-reflection. It can guide you to identify relationships between two things that don't exist or to overestimate the level which two things are connected. This is a cognitive bias referred to as illusory correlation.

Ask the correct self-reflection question

Instead of asking why questions, try to ask questions that will help you concentrate on goals or solutions. To achieve that, start to ask 'what' questions. These questions include, "What am I feeling right now?" instead of, "Why do I feel so bad?" If you think this way, you will start to name your emotions, which will then reduce the negative attitudes and feelings.

Additionally, avoid asking yourself a problem-centred question. Don't ask, "What challenges am I facing right now?" But frame the question around a goal, you can ask, "What would I like my relationship with my boss to be like a month from now?" Counsellors and coaches are discovering that solution-focused questions tend to make clients feel good, while problem-focused questions make clients feel less satisfied.

If you are going through a constant problem on your mind, ask yourself questions that will change your focus to potential solutions. These can be as straightforward as, "What it is one potential solution to this problem?" and then, "What is one method that I could begin to move forward building this solution?"

Applying solution-focused questions has two advantages:

1. It uncovers possible answers to the problems.

2. It boosts your confidence in your ability to solve future dilemmas.

A feeling of agency and control impacts your sense of confidence, boosts your self-worth, and raises the odds you will stick to your intentions.

Why is self-awareness difficult

Purchasing a self-help book or finding an inspiration guru can provide you with a quick feeling that you are doing something about your problems. But self-awareness requires that you look for time to address your issues by yourself.

While there are many benefits of creating self-awareness, the practice requires time. Fortunately, that time is free and available to use if we plan.

Rather than go for easy solutions, find time to sit down and think. Set aside 15 minutes for reflecting into your daily-or at least weekly routine. Try to make time for reflecting your first activity of the day. Keep your phone away, and wait to switch on your computer, attach a "do not disturb" sign on your monitor, and give yourself that 15 minutes to think.

You might need to become creative with the way you organize your day so you can find sense in uninterrupted time.

Of course, the answers to all your issues cannot be found within you. There's probably the right time for research. However, taking time to think and reflect can assist you to narrow down the few questions where you require more information instead of ruminating.

Chapter 3: Boost Your Emotional Intelligence

Learning to recognize emotions

It is a known fact that feelings are an essential aspect of our lives, but the problem is that many of us have been raised to override emotions. Childhood messages play a significant role in creating this state of mind. We feel guilty if we disclose our feelings of anger, guilt, annoyance and shame. We are afraid that we will hurt the emotions of others because we want to please others. The outcome of this suppression is always anxiety, depression, restlessness, and phobias.

People acquire a negative and pessimistic attitude in life. Feelings are generally complicated and it is hard to identify them. Sometimes, even if we recognize them, it becomes difficult to express them. It is crucial to identify feelings and then be able to show them well to avoid the dangers of being prone to phobias and anxiety.

Before we can learn to identify emotions, it is important to understand the different types of emotions that we experience daily and try to look at them from a new dimension.

Every negative emotion we experience every day can guide us to make the right decisions throughout the day. Therefore, we must take some time to learn to understand, recognize, and interpret our emotions in methods that will help us identify answers to the issues we face.

Uncovering types of human emotions

Before we start to look at these emotions, it is critical that you understand that these emotional responses are a sign to your conscious brain that something isn't working, and hence, something needs to change. In other words, they are an indicator that you need to do something specific to eliminate your pain.

Lastly, all these emotions occur because of stuck-states that we let happen to us. These stuck-states can be said to be patterned responses to people, events, and situations that have their own physiological words, answers and, etc.

Let us now explore these emotional states.

Fear

Fear is a debilitating emotion that results in anxiety, indecision and worry.

You experience fear because you interpret a situation in a way that results in a feeling of dread. This feeling of awe leads to an emotional response to what may happen in future if you take a certain action.

Fear can be a good thing if it's something that depends on hard facts and evidence that is meant to protect you from danger. But most of the times our fears are filled with inaccuracies that mislead us. As a result, the first step you need to take to eliminate anxiety from your life is to separate the "real" from the "imagined."

Of course, fear is a critical emotion because it secures us from harm in the off-chance that we are escaping from danger. But in most cases, the fear we experience hurts us because it prevents us from realizing our objectives and goals.

Here are some quick things that you need to do to control your fears effectively. First, you need to make it clear what it is you want. Secondly, be ready with the actions you will take to resolve your desired results. These steps are important because most of our fears depend on the lack of knowledge and lack of preparation.

Anger

You are angry because you interpret a situation in a way that naturally makes you experience anger. But anger can serve us if we can understand its hidden meaning.

However, before you can embrace the emotion of anger, it is important to understand that rage always occurs because one or more of our rules has been violated by others. For that reason, we are angry because we don't feel in control of a given situation, or circumstances. In this case, we can let go of anger quite fast by taking time to re-evaluate the rules. Maybe they aren't reasonable, perhaps they are out-of-date, or they just should not be used in these situations.

In the same way, anger can happen because of an incorrect interpretation of a situation. In the following case, you need to determine whether or not you have misinterpreted a job or misinterpreted people's intentions. In the following example, remain open to the possibilities and search for alternative meanings. It is only an open and flexible method that will offer you the answers you want.

Guilt

You could be feeling guilty if you consider a situation in a way that makes you feel guilty. And the longer you feel guilty, the more it continues to grow inside your head.

When you feel guilty, remember it is because of your interpretation of an incident, you did that you failed, and the effect this has had on others. Once you interpret events of your life in a unique way, it is the time guilt changes and becomes something that can inspire you and empower you to take affirmative action.

Convince your mind that the impact your actions have had on others is not as you think.

Guilt is resolved when you can make peace with yourself and the people you might have hurt.

Inadequacy

Inadequacy can cause you to feel miserable and incompetent. It is an emotion that makes you feel like you are at the bottom of the heap without a way out.

You might feel inadequate if you don't have the experience, knowledge, and skills to live up to your high expectations. Therefore, you can change your expectations about yourself and your ability, or you can step out and gain the right skills, knowledge, and experience required to achieve the results you want in your life.

You might be feeling inadequate because you undermine your strengths and abilities. In this case, it's important to get a second opinion. As a result, get out and ask someone for feedback. Tell them to give their honest observations. Maybe they will offer you with surprising perspectives and insight.

Lastly, inadequacy can always emerge from a lack of confidence. If you have low self-esteem, then it looks okay to feel inadequate. But if you take the time to grow your faith, then you will increase your self-belief and start to feel better about yourself and your prospects.

Disappointment

You become disappointed when you don't get what you want and always arises from a sense-of-defeat.

You can be disappointed because you interpret a situation in a way that makes you feel disappointed. Rather than look for answers and solutions, you are stuck in a muddy pit of unfulfilled objectives, goals and dreams that never became a reality.

When you feel disappointed, we normally wish that things could be different. However, regardless of how hard we try, we cannot reverse the past, but we can change our experience in a positive manner.

Rather than wallow in disappointment, choose to learn from your experiences so that you can better yourself in the future. Sometimes, it is even important to look for opportunities that could now be available because of the disappointment that you have experienced.

Disappointment is the result of having unfulfilled goals; if that's the case then you may have to adjust your objectives to make them more achievable. That way, you are less likely to feel disappointed.

Overwhelm

Overwhelm is an emotion that enters your body over time, and before you realize it, it traps your whole life and can result in depression and grief.

You are feeling overwhelmed because you have a lot on your plate or you are unable to take control of features of your life. In this case, you feel-out-of-control and unable to respond well.

The answer lies in taking back control over small steps of your life. It involves taking part of your life and dividing it up into smaller, manageable sections that you can complete.

It also means letting go of any unnecessary commitments that are pulling you down or rescheduling then in a manner that will free up your time while providing you with enough space to do what is critical.

Resolving to overwhelm is easy if you know what to do and are ready to take the actions necessary to reprioritize and reschedule your life accordingly. Sometimes, all you need to do is a little lesson in productivity.

Frustration

This is one of those emotions that we don't want to experience because it makes us feel like we are so close, yet so far away from the result, we want.

You experience frustration because you interpret a situation in a way that makes you feel frustrated. It is within this feeling that your answers lie.

You could be frustrated because you are striving to do something, but you seem not to get the results that you want. It is like you are being prevented from realizing your goal by an external force that you cannot control.

Rather than attempt to control the situation, the secret is to start thinking outside the box; to start thinking of new possibilities, and possible solutions that could help you solve the problem you are working with. Sometimes, all you need to do is to search for further information that will generate insight you need to see the situation from a different perspective.

Lastly, frustration results from not finding the results you are after. In this case, all you need to do to resolve your failures is to change your approach. Try something new and different that you have never thought of before. Determination, curiosity, and flexible approach are the goals that you need to be looking for.

Loneliness

Loneliness can be a dangerous emotion that results in sadness and staginess'.

You feel lonely because you look at life in a way that alienates you from everyone.

The key to dealing with loneliness is to reconnect with others, to reconnect with your environment, and with a higher cause that will allow you to feel fulfilled and passionate about your life.

Loneliness grows within our hearts because we forget all the things that we are thankful for.

That said, let us jump to how to identify and express your emotions.

Withheld feelings manifest through different types of bodily and psychological symptoms. For instance, anxiety can be caused by the anticipation of a negative result. Worried individuals are always insecure and fear bad things might happen to them. There talk always highlighted by, "what if?" type and this results in anxiety. Feelings have a charge of energy, but we usually try to hide that energy and do not want to reveal our emotions.

Sometimes, when we hide our feelings of sadness for a long time, we feel depressed. When we release our feelings by crying and talking, we feel relieved.

Research shows that holding onto anger for a long time without expressing it can cause depression. We also experience psychosomatic symptoms when we suppress our emotions for a long time. Symptoms such as blood pressure, cardiac problems could be because of suppressing feelings. When you master how to recognize your beliefs, you can limit the symptoms of psychosomatic illness.

Also, when you suppress your emotions, it can cause tension in the muscle groups. Anger can be suppressed by tightening different muscles from the eyes to the pelvis. Fear can be suppressed by tightening muscle group in the stomach and the area around the diaphragm. You can withhold anger by stretching the back of your neck and shoulders. To eliminate the tension in these muscle groups, you must learn to apply muscle relaxation technique.

How you can tune your body

As said before, we like to hold our feelings in different parts of the body. It is critical to optimize your body to recognize your feelings. Here are steps you can take to tune your body.

1. Physically relax for 5-10 minutes, to slow down your mind.
2. Now ask yourself, "How am I feeling right now?"
3. Tune in to that part in your body where you feel emotional sensations like sadness, anger and fear. This is your secret place of feelings.
4. Wait and pay attention to whatever you can sense in your place of feelings. Do not judge but become an observer. If you start to examine, then you might not find a sense of your actual feeling.

If we fail to take control of our emotions or identify reasons why we're feeling them, then they'll continue to disturb our minds-even when they are not important. That could hurt our health, relationships and success.

Transforming your emotional state

It is okay to understand what exactly emotions represent, but in the event, we are caught up; the first reaction is always an emotional reaction that has a habit of working against us instead for us. In this case, you need to be aware of a moving state transformation process, which we discuss below.

1. Recognize your emotions

The first step in emotional state transformation is to recognize your feeling. You must know the kind of emotions you are experiencing. This is critical because if you aren't sure of the type of emotion you experience, then you will find a hard time to respond accordingly.

To assist you to overcome this step, try to ask yourself these two questions:

- How am I feeling now?
- Do I always feel this way, or there is something more?

The clearer you become, the more you will have to strive as you move through this process.

2. Understand your emotion

It is important at this stage that regardless of what feeling you experience that you do not resist it. Resistance will only create uncertainty and prevent you from turning this emotion into something you can use to work with as you move on.

It is therefore imperative that you openly appreciate the emotion that you experience and look for its meaning and significance in the state that you find yourself in.

For example, if something suddenly makes you angry, acknowledge that you are feeling angry, and these events have made you angry.

Only when you can acknowledge this emotion openly will be ready to move forward to the next step.

3. Analyze your emotion

The most critical thing that you need to do at this stage is to be curious. Curiosity will provide a channel for a new opportunity that can help you develop unique insights into your emotion and the situation you find yourself in.

To help you increase your level of curiosity concerning the emotion you experience, ask yourself these questions:

What do I gain from this emotion?

What should I do to make things better?

What is the correct value of this emotion?

What do I desire?

How can I learn from this to become better in the future?

Keep in mind that regardless of the type of emotion you experience, it is there to help you in some way. To learn important lessons about yourself, your situations and about life in general. Therefore, be open and search for the correct answers that will allow you to gain insights needed to overcome this emotional obstacle you are working through.

4. Be confident that you can handle the emotion

This is the moment to be confident and select the emotional response you will experience moving forward. It is also the time to acquire any relevant knowledge and support that you may need that will help you to control your response effectively.

To help with the following process, it is important to remember a time in your past where you dealt with this emotion successfully. This memory can be applied as the foundation that will make way for a bright future where you are no longer controlled by this emotion, but consciously decide to respond to this emotion in a useful and proactive manner.

5. Take the necessary action

Now that you have all the information you need to respond in a constructive and robust way, it is time to take a proactive action to change your emotional state for the better.

How to take charge of your emotional state?

For you to boost your resilience in awkward moments, it is important to spend time building your emotional fortress.

Emotional stress is a place you turn to keep you strong during tough moments.

Within this emotional stress, you can meet and talk with your peers.

Also, your emotional fortress has several self-improvement resources that you can apply to boost your resolve. All these resources and support connections are there for you to allow you develop the upper-hand once you face the challenges.

Learn to use your emotional stress during moments of high emotional difficulty where you need that extra support to guide you in the right direction. Rather than react emotionally in restricting ways to the events and circumstances in your life, take some time to remove yourself from your situations and enter your emotional fortress, which will provide you with the answers and guide you to respond in a positive and optimal manner.

Breath control

Anytime you are feeling emotionally under the weather; it is essential to calm yourself by breathing consciously. Breath-in for five counts, and exhale for five more counts, while maintaining paying attention to your breath.

Repeat this process for up to five minutes at a time, and you will quickly discover a new vigour and energy that you can apply to think clearly and effectively about the situations you are being confronted with.

Psychological transformation

Your expectations, thoughts, and perceptions work together to create the reality you want every day.

However, they all come together and affect the emotions you experience at any time.

Therefore, you must select your thoughts consciously, and change your expectations of circumstances in positive ways. You are making them work for you instead of against you.

Whatever you take in your mind grow as the day goes. Whether you like it or not, it will affect how you perceive reality. So you must ensure you choose what will enhance positive emotional growth to help you optimize your day and the choices that are presented to you.

Express your needs and desires

One of the most effective methods to break down emotional turmoil is to communicate your wishes to others.

Most of the time, our communication is reduced, which results in misunderstandings and disagreement. This leads to emotional mayhem and turmoil. To fix this, ask others to determine how they feel, why they are feeling that way and how they would prefer to resolve these feelings. Similarly, communicate your desires in the same way.

Sometimes, open communication and a readiness to listen, to resolve any emotional conflict that you may experience throughout your day.

Eye movements

Lastly, it is important to highlight that in numerous ways, human emotions are connected to the eye movement. This means that when we are going through a certain emotion our eyes move in a given direction that signals to the brain that we are now, experiencing the emotion of depression.

In summary, always remember that it is not what happens to you that matters, but the way you respond to the events and challenges of lives that makes all the difference in the end.

You are always in control of your emotions regardless of how things may look. Therefore, you can decide to feel differently and to take conscious control of your emotional state.

Practical ways to improve your emotional intelligence

Emotional Intelligence refers to your ability to perceive your own emotions, plus the emotions of other people, and control them in a healthy and productive manner.

Emotional intelligence is critical to our life experience and affects how successful we are in our relationships and careers. Regardless of the stage of life, you are, you can apply these simple steps to boost your emotional intelligence and increase your self-awareness and empathy.

The benefits of having a higher emotional intelligence are many. Emotional intelligence sometimes referred to as EQ, positively affects your self-esteem, your mental health, your job performance, and the quality of your relationships.

While high emotional intelligence is not a mandatory need to succeed in life, it is useful in different places. One can argue that emotional intelligence is increasingly valuable as our world becomes more and more automated and robotic. Human beings have started to crave for more and more authentic emotional connection more than ever.

No matter what, you were born with a naturally lower EQ set point, or you were more emotionally wired in your life, and it was attuned in you, everyone can boost their emotional intelligence if they are ready to put in a little effort.

Here are some things that you can do to boost your emotional intelligence.

1. Slow down and experience your feelings

When exhausting or challenging emotions occur, the default human response is to get busy doing more work or temporarily deaden the emotions by applying maladaptive numbing behavior.

Rather than distract yourself, slow down, and allow yourself to experience your feelings fully.

If you feel anxious, accept that you feel anxious. If you experience heaviness of grief within your chest, let it be there. If you have to cry, then cry.

Sit it with it calmly and patiently, and let the emotion speak to you.

Don't rationalize or judge your emotions. Let it come up as they are. Keep in mind; you are trying to get out of your head and into your heart. Allow it to take time to establish the bridge to connect the two.

Slowing down and allowing your feelings is the first and most effective tool to increase your self-awareness.

2. Communicate your challenging emotions to important people

There will be moments when you are so occupied by your feelings that it will be difficult to know what is happening inside of you. Or there could be moments where, when you are first building a new emotional self-awareness, a new feeling arises for you that you don't understand.

In these moments, it is important to confide in a safe and loving person who you can open up your feelings. Tell them as much as you can, and let them reflect you what they are seeing about your emotional experience.

3. Learn to trust yourself as time goes

Boosting your emotional intelligence requires time. This is not something that can happen overnight. It is about learning to trust yourself and your review of your emotional reality and the realities of others.

Although it is important to open to others feedback about you, don't take their word as truer than your internal perception of yourself. Overall, you are learning to trust yourself more and what you feel yourself is the truth.

Don't make your feelings wrong for existing. Just accept them as they are, even if they don't make sense.

4. Learn to decrease negative emotions

Have you ever felt depressed? Or stressed?

Stress can be said to be the accumulation of unfelt feelings.

Do you have a bunch of sadness, anger, resentment, or frustration that you haven't dealt with? As it continues to pile up, you start to feel the cumulative effects of stress.

It is difficult to differentiate what you are feeling if there is a lot of internal stimuli accumulating inside you.

It becomes vital that you learn to reduce stress through emotional processing.

5. Pay attention to your internal and external reactions to others

One quick way to boost your emotional intelligence is to begin being aware of the reactions that you have to others.

Then, let those reactions inform you of your emotional defaulting patterns.

For instance, if you find yourself angry by people who cut you off in traffic, are rude to people, or are always late, then allow yourself to look at those emotions as they develop. Understand your default emotional state when it comes to responding to others.

Once you discover your small handful of most constantly used emotional responses, it will become easier to identify and control those same emotions later on.

6. Practice emotional management

Once you understand your emotions and that of others, it is critical to know how to balance them and keep it in check. Some methods of practising emotional management comprise:

- Divert your attention until you feel composed
- Look at the big picture and determine how important the immediate reaction is to the general problem.
- Re-frame the experience, i.e. explore broader means of looking at the problem.
- Divert your attention until you feel composed.

7. Create connections with other people

Regardless of how introverted or shy, you think you are, learning how to build networks with others is a great aspect of Emotional Intelligence.

Even if you feel shy, you can start first by listening, showing interest, and making others feel comfortable. Doing so is easier for shy, introverted persons than it is for extroverts who like to enjoy speaking first. For both types, revealing that you care and are interested in others goes far in creating valuable connections.

Boosting your emotional intelligence takes time. It all comes down to mindfulness. Improving emotional intelligence is determined by you slowing down, and slowly becoming aware of yourself and others.

How to fully eliminate difficult emotions that tend to hold you back

Do your emotions generate trouble in your life?

If you have lived for more than a decade, the odds are high that there are some emotions inside you that hold you back in your life.

You might not be consciously aware of these challenging emotions on a daily basis…. But they are affecting you and eating your emotional bandwidth that could be used for more lightness, joy, and bliss.

It could be that your unprocessed emotions show up as anger towards your friends, or judgment towards people you don't know.

Your challenging emotions restrict you from doing anything in every part of your life. They are toxic in your subconscious mind.

They interfere with the way you connect with others, how you present yourself sexually, and in the amount of happiness that you experience every day.

And it is not your fault. You have been motivated to repress your emotions. And when you are emotionally suppressed, you are an easier target to sell to. Society tends to make sure you feel stuck and unhappy.

However, once you access your stuck emotional energy and feeling your way through it, you will have the freedom and permission to live without your old emotional residue.

If you take part in this process, even just a handful of times in the next month, you will discover a relevant and general feeling of weightlessness. Physical tension will disappear out of your body, and your relationship will increase overnight.

Gaining access to your suppressed emotions

If your emotions are conditioned, not to expect that they can get your attention, it will require time for them to trust you again.

Simply because you have the intention of wanting to feel your feelings, doesn't imply that they will all avail themselves to you for you to process your way through them.

This process will take time. And the longer it has been since you were consistently emotionally authentic with yourself, the more time it will take for your emotions to surrender themselves to you.

Check out these methods to coax repressed emotions

1. Eliminate distractions

Find a sacred place for your emotional processing.

Turn of any electronic device, or anything that might interfere with your energetic space. Select a time when you know that you will dive into your feelings without interference.

2. Become still

For the emotional chaos to feel safe enough to bubble up to the surface, you need to be physically still.

Emotions pass through softened bodies.

Whether you are sitting comfortably or lying down is up to you. Just ensure that you are in a relaxed position and your major muscle groups are not tensed up.

3. Breathe deeply

Take advantage of your breath to connect your mind to your body. Breathe deeply and expand your breath into every section of your body. As you do this, you may find places in your body where you were holding physical tension.

Soften your shoulders. Allow your tongue to disconnect from the roof of your mouth. Relax your legs fully.

Breath your full breath into every inch of your body, and begin to feel what bubbles up for you, without judging whatever you discover.

4. Determine the location of your emotions in your body

At this point, you might begin to discover areas that are more intense than others or specific emotions that you might be able to name by feeling them.

You could discover things such as, "I feel anxious in my throat," or "I feel anger in my chest."

Whatever you discover, bad or good. It simply is.

If you can, name your findings to validate your findings outside of your mind.

5. Thank them

Now, with whatever emotions you discover, thank them for being there and for letting you be aware of them.

As always, you want to speak something in a manner that makes sense to you.

You could say something like, "I appreciate for letting me witness you, sadness," or "Thank you for revealing yourself to my anger."

You can even go further by saying, "You have a home here," or "You can stay for as long as you need to, my beautiful friend."

The point is to accept the emotion into your body the way you would welcome a guest that you are happy to see with kindness, grace, and compassion.

How you can process and heal your difficult emotions

Once you ascertain and name the emotions that you have treasure-hunted in your body, it is time to begin expanding them and letting them move through you.

And keep in mind, if you are at a stage in your emotional journey where the details of what the emotions are not clear to you yet, that is still fine.

You don't have to be able to name an emotion to feel it. The following steps will help you in increasing the emotion to a more significant state, and, hence, it might be clear what it is throughout the process.

1. Support them to be bigger

Now that you have connected with the emotions in your body, it is the moment to begin encouraging them to grow inside of you.

The only means to let your emotions move through your body is to accept that they are there and to motivate them to have your complete attention for a moment in time. It is the resistance that the emotions live inside of you that has prevented them for so long.

Motivate them to be bigger by saying things such as kindly show me more, thank you, or it is okay to reveal me more of this sadness.

Again, talk to the emotions like they are an old, trusted friend. Be gentle and supportive, and let them grow in you, if only by letting it grow 5% at a time.

2. Breathe them into more fullness

If you feel like you can only persuade the emotions out using words and encouraging terms to a specific low ceiling, then it could be the moment to breathe them into more fullness.

Breathe deeply while consciously releasing your emotions to the whole body. For instance, if you are feeling anxious in your stomach and throat, then mentally let your anxiety to consume your whole torso, and then your whole body. Give it full authority to take you over while you surrender to it fully.

Keep in mind, and no emotion is permanent. Even when this particular exercise leads to temporary discomfort, it will be worth it because you will have let the emotion to have all your attention, after which it will properly vanish from you once and for all.

3. Say to them, "thank you, kindly show me more."

Continue to shift deep breaths with supportive words. Continue to expand the emotion in the entire body.

"You have a home here jealousy, sadness, or grief, etc. Show me more. What would even more of this emotion feel like?

4. Move your body

In case sitting or lying down makes you feel too stuck, you are allowed to stand up, move your body around, and will enable the emotion to move you as it needs to.

This is also the best stage to practice trauma so that your body can begin to shake out its physical tension.

If you have not heard of trauma releases exercises, it is important when you intentionally let your body induce tremoring to release old buried stress and tension. The easiest method to do this is to lie flat on your back with your feet touching and your knees spread apart. Then, slowly bring your knees together until they begin to shake and maintain your legs in that position so that tremoring continues.

5. Keep breathing

Remember, whether you are doing Trauma release exercise, or verbally supporting your emotions to expand in your body, or lying down and bawling your eyes out, keep breathing deeply. Your conscious breathing supports the movement of the emotions to continue to move throughout your body.

6. Let your emotions remain there without judging them

If you are overwhelmed by anger and you want to hit your pillow against your bed, go for it. If you have to scream into a pillow with frustration, that is supported. If you have to hold yourself, and sob uncontrollably, that is okay.

Whatever it is you feel, it is okay. Just allow the emotions to remain there without judgment.

There is no right way to carry out this exercise. Your process will always be interrupted by an incoming emotion... but it is never interrupted. The point of this general process is to let whatever the feelings are that come up.

If you feel happy, they feel happy. If you feel sad, then let yourself feel sad. There is no right channel, and there is no failure. Just stick to whatever comes up, as it comes up.

Your only goal is to let your emotions happen.

What you should do after your feelings

After some time, it might feel like your emotional processing session has completed its course. Whether you have been feeling your feelings for five minutes or five hours is irrelevant. The fact that you have been self-loving even to try to feel your repressed emotions is enough.

Below are some important loving steps you can take to honor yourself after your emotional processing.

1. Clean your tears

Or allow them to dry on your face.

2. Be gentle

Take a bubble bath. Take some dark chocolate. Lie down for a nap. Wrap yourself in your best soft blanket. Sink into your best self-care practices.

Whatever your heart directs you is the most self-honoring and self-compassionate step with the best course of action you can take.

3. Journal your experience, and discuss it with a close friend you trust.

Did a new lesson emerge for you during your emotional processing? Did you discover the root causes of your suffering? Did a painful memory emerge for you?

Take notes in your diary, cell phone's notepad for future reference.

4. Take action on anything that you might have learned about yourself

Have you ever thought of someone you wanted to apologize regarding your past actions? Did you recognize that some critical aspects of your life, job, health, and habits are out of alignment?

If new plans of action were availed to you, now could be the right time to take action on whatever you have learned. And in case the realizations tend to be extra world-changing, then you might have to sleep on your newfound action plan and wait until you wake up in a better state.

How to respond and not react

Whether you are talking to family, romantic partners, or even coworkers or employees, the way you communicate is critical, especially when it is about a serious topic. But how can you become a considerate communicator?

It all begins with how you listen, to be a good listener, you need to actively pay attention to what the other individual is saying, trying to understand their perspective, and accepting their feelings and thoughts, instead of hearing what they say and waiting for your opportunity to talk. But beyond that, there's one small thing you can remember-the difference between responding to something and reacting to something.

If you are thinking to yourself, "aren't those the same thing?" you are not fully wrong. They are connected, but there is a difference that can fully change the direction of a conversation. A reaction is sudden, emotional, and depends on your beliefs, and biases, and from your unconscious mind. On the other hand, a response originates slowly, depending on the information from both your conscious and unconscious mind. That means reactions are always defensive or survival-based, and you could regret them later, while responses are more considerate of more than one perspective.

In other words, a response is an action that depends on logic, while a reaction is an emotional state. Sometimes, both response and reaction may appear the same, the intention behind them, and the results that follow them can be different.

Consider what you'd face when broaching a serious, or difficult topic of conversation. Would you rather the other individual react immediately with all of their emotions, or would you rather take time to consider your point of view and take time to think it before giving your response?

The latter looks more appealing.

To become more mindful, remember that small difference in mind and actively challenge yourself to respond more than you react. You may realize that conflicts are more easily resolved, and tough talks go a little smoother.

Tips to help you respond than react

    1. Be present and recognize what you are doing

Awareness is the difference between responding and reacting. Being aware that you are about to react in a manner that is unbecoming and having the potential to stop yourself before you do it. Mindful awareness provides you with a means to track your automatic reactions so that you can stop them before they are destructive. This skill can be developed through regular mindfulness because it will allow you to get used to understanding what it feels like just before you do something you haven't given much thought to.

The perfect way to practice this is meditating, and there are many different types, so you need to identify one that works for you, whether you are a new or a veteran.

2. Remove tension in socially acceptable ways

When you choose to react instead of respond, it is because you have a lot of energy, in most cases, negative energy. When you bottle up those emotions regularly, they finally build-up to the level where an explosion is hard to control. The easiest solution to this challenge is to make sure you have socially acceptable methods of removing tension while it is still in small levels. That way, you will remain calm and respond in a level-headed way.

Some excellent exercises you can do to remove tension include:

- Controlled breathing. In this exercise, you count how long it will take to breathe in, hold and release air from your lungs, or control it such that each one takes a specific amount of time. A common exercise is to breathe in for 4 seconds, hold it for 7 seconds, and breathe out for 8 seconds. This is meant to calm you down better than any other length of time.

Similarly, you can concentrate on your breathing without counting, but focus on what it feels and sounds like. This diverts your mind from your emotions while at the same time training your brain to focus and recognize how things feel in the moment.

- Body scan, tense, and release: In this exercise, you sit or lay in a comfortable state and take your time to concentrate on every muscle group. As you continue to feel your muscles, you should tighten and release the tension and notice how relaxed it feels afterward. Do this, until you have scanned, tensed and released every single muscle in your body.

- Sprint and walk

Jog lightly, and burst into a sprint at a great speed for 10 seconds. After that, walk slowly as you can for 30 seconds. During this sprint, notice the way your body feels, and notice the difference while walking. You can do this thing while lifting weights at the gym. All you need to do is to determine the difference between how your body experiences while it's experiencing full physical tension and the way it feels when that tension is no longer there. This will allow you to identify where your emotions are making your muscles tense, and you can relieve them instantly.

3. Learn to pause

Pausing before you act is the main ground of responding. Reacting takes place instantly. There is no room for forethought. Therefore, if you can learn to put yourself that reaction on hold, even if it is only for a split second, you will be teaching your brain to stop and think for longer periods in the future.

A better way to practice pausing is learning to count to 3 before responding to any question, regardless of that question or who is asking it. The little pause will not affect the quality of your conversation, but it will provide you with time to come up with a well-thought-out response.

Alternatively, you can ask yourself a question. Your brain will probably take time to respond to that question in your head, providing you the time to respond. So you can as well make that question part of the exercise. Ask things like "What would be the most compassionate response be in these cases?" or "How can I respond in a way that reflects my goals for this relationship?"

4. Add a filter

Assume a water filter. As water from your pipes flows through the filtered sediment and other unwanted factors get trapped in it, the water becomes pure and fresh. This is something that you can do with your reactions. By defining rules for yourself and dedicating to them, you will provide your brain with the responsibility to know when you are breaking those rules.

The rule you set for your mental filter is not to allow any complaints flow through your consciousness and make it out of your mouth. So any moment you use a phrase that is close to a complaint, your brain will remove it. In some cases, it will slip through, but over time you catch it halfway. Finally, you will recognize it and stop it altogether before you open your mouth.

5. List down your fears and assumptions

Labeling what you are feeling takes more mental effort than you might expect. To name an emotion, you have first to identify the effect that emotion is having on your physical body, the feeling it is sending through your senses.

You have to determine what is causing it and which assumption you had was proven wrong to activate this feeling. All this requires time and the time it takes you to consider all these things will cool you down and stop you from reacting because it will consume the mental resources needed to react in the first place.

Another aspect is that once you identify what you are feeling and why you can begin to determine how to correct the problem productively. Putting what you are going through into words in your head will allow you to express it to a different person and that person might help you make things better. You must be honest with yourself about what you are feeling, even if it is uncomfortable to comfort. It is the only means to heal.

6. Request for what you want

This is similar to labeling your feelings. For you to exactly ask what you want, you have to realize what it is you want. That is easier said than done, because of the time we feel like we have a need that is too vague to say and if we cannot reveal it we certainly cannot satisfy it. Thinking about what it is you want will consume time to allow you to relax and respond with consideration.

Be sure that once you ask for what you want and that you also ask if the other person is ready to provide it. If not, find out what they are ready to do or what you could do to assist them in meeting you halfway. It is more productive than shouting at them or crying.

7. Maintain the situation in context

Having every situation in context is critical. The reason is that anything can be frustrating when interrupted out of context. And there's no reason in overreacting to something that is not a threat. If you hear footsteps of a person walking at night, it could be that somebody has broken into your house or it could imply your partner has finally come back from working the night shift. Understanding the context sets the difference between you reacting with fear or responding with calm satisfaction. Always reflect on what is happening and how the current situation can affect you're going forward.

8. Retain the big picture in mind

When you understand how each situation suits your overall goals and objectives, it becomes easy to respond. Zooming out allows you to discover how the little things can help or prevent your efforts. As long as you understand where you are going, how you arrive there is not a big deal. But you need to be clear on your important values, or you could find yourself frustrated when conflict arises.

9. Ask yourself the main question

Sometimes all you need to do is to ask yourself whether you are reacting or responding. This will give you time to pause and processes all the available information to understand the answer to your question. This split-second might be all the time you need to take a mental break from the incident and select an alternate route.

10. Understand that you always have a choice

Most of the time, we react when we feel like we have no choice. When we feel like we have lost control over the situation our mind plays tricks on us and makes us see that there is no way to get what we want. But we understand that's not true. Regardless of what kind of situation you are in, there is always a way to deal with it. And realizing this can empower. When you feel motivated you are likely to prefer the option with the least possible negative result.

Chapter 4: Improve your leadership skills

Get Organized

As an entrepreneur, you need to be alert to the next opportunity that might arise. But that can be difficult if you have a lot of unscheduled appointments, meetings that take long, junk email messages, or a messy office. There are different techniques and products highlighted as the solution to making your time more productive and your life organized, but who has the time to compare them, or even learn how to use them?

The good news is that you can take control of your business life instead of letting it take control of you, and you may not have to spend a dollar. All you need is a small investment of time, to build your own system for monitoring track of the critical things while filtering everything else that gets in the way. These guidelines can allow you to develop your personalized path to productivity.

Although a clattered desk might not be a sign of a cluttered mind, it will not help you to stay organized and be ready for success.

1. Set realistic goals and remain focused

Your goals are directions that you will follow day in and day out to attain the success you want. Make sure that they are realistic and inspiring, and keep them constantly front of mind so you will be reminded to maintain your focus on realizing them.

2. Look for a calendar, and maintain it, always

Whether it is an old-fashioned desk calendar or the modern synced-across-ten-devices app based, the fact is to use it religiously. If you find yourself back to writing appointments on sticky notes, that is a good sign you are losing focus.

3. Clean your workstation

It is challenging to stay organized and on top of your crucial tasks and priorities when your desk or office is a mess. Spend an hour or two every week to arrange the paperwork that is consuming every inch of surface area. File away things you don't need and take the necessary action on the things that require it.

4. Organize your priorities

Complete your top priorities first and lowest priorities last.

5. Don't let your inbox control you

So try to check your inbox the first thing in the morning and later in the day for critical messages. When checking your inbox, scan the inbox for items that can be handled immediately. For example, unsolicited mail, appointments and so on.

Don't be scared to delete the key before you open the message. And once you open the message read it, delegate it or respond immediately. In case a comprehensive response is required, or you decide to take on an action move the message to a task list.

6. Review your list

Ensure you check your list every day. Find out what needs doing and by when. Add notes to the tasks and take pleasure in setting the completed flag when you complete your work. Additionally, spend some time at the end of the week to monitor your progress and be ready for the next.

7. Communicate

Finally, whatever you do, the best way to stay organized as a leader is to communicate. How are you moving on? What milestone have you achieved? What is pulling you behind? Are you going to hit the deadline?

Develop a constant communication schedule, this can be sending an update email at the end of the week or daily on important projects that need to be done first. Set a reminder on your calendar or phone for yourself and provide a quick summary.

Being organized does not mean that you can do it all, but it can assist you to make clear your expectations of what is possible. Apply these tips to get into some regular habits of how you want to track your tasks, and how you want to keep those around you updated.

It is not always about doing more, but is about doing what you like doing well, and ensuring important people are aware about it, which will help you stay ahead in any organization.

Self-Development Tips

Self-improvement is a great term that directly refers to the act of improving yourself. It can consist of personal development based on goal setting, organizational skills, time management, leadership skills, visualization skills, and mind power.

Self-improvement tips allow persons of any age to overcome negative and unwanted thoughts that prevent them from thinking in themselves.

Also, this term allows you to convert your negative thoughts into beliefs that motivate and encourage yourself. It can assist you to make positive and significant changes in each aspect of your life. The self-improvement process generates many benefits.

This section will help you learn more about self-development and tips you can apply.

Essential benefits

Self-development tips allow professionals to understand their professional limitations, which can help them focus on improving. Therefore, one can effectively grow their talents and skills for their own benefit. Alongside this, self-improvement goals allow you to select a new hobby, skills or interest which are important for living a good life. Through a self-development tips process, you can easily select the mistakes in how you always work in your office, or working environment. This will allow you to make positive efforts that will be relevant for improving your professionalism. Self-improvement tips not only increase your confidence level but also allow you to achieve your professional goal fast.

Self-development tips

There are various self-improvement tips available to boost yourself, but the right one helps you to achieve numerous benefits. If you want to attain those stunning ideas, you can keep reading. These self-improvement tips will help you kick start your individual development endeavors. For you to realize the new range of satisfaction, you need to include the self-improvement tips into your daily life. The personal development deals with all the important self-improvement tricks that will inspire your progression. It also enhances your self-confidence and delivers amazing results.

1. Expect to achieve

Many people believe that individuals who are winning in this world are smarter than them, but it is not a must. The real tip is to anticipate winning earlier than it has happened. This method doesn't stress sufficiently how important this is, because your mindset is made up of a powerful effect on not or whether you will realize your self-improvement dreams and goals. Understand that it never says you need self-improvement skills to accomplish, because the fact of the matter is having a determined and bold hope is more than having the effective skills. It will basically come with persistence and conviction.

2. Daily affirmations

Cultivating a great practice of reading distinctly positive affirmations daily will change your personality and character. Along with this, it also changes the activities you can take every day of your life. Most people discovered that applying this tip when they wake up and before they go to sleep work extremely well.

If you want to attain the important benefits, you need to adhere to this powerful habit in a regular manner. You cannot help but create the inner self effectively by adhering to this self-improvement idea daily. The constant practice will create the right results within the shortest duration.

3. Write down specific goals and action plan

The simple act of putting your pen to a piece of paper involves a theatrical effect on easily specifying your aid and career goals with the expectation you discover above. The routine practice of writing goals is important when you want to achieve your self-improvement goals soon. Dreaming is a great thing and doing is another powerful thing. Every written objective should guide you to the distinctive long-term objective and amazing life. This remarkable idea will help you improve your skills and personality in a better way. Along with this, it also plays a critical role in the self-improvement skills process, so you can follow without any problems.

4. Highlight your blind spots

Most people attempt to accomplish their self-development tips, but they fail to achieve because of some reasons. If you want to discover the main causes, keep reading this self-improvement tip. Scientifically, blind spots are defined as the sections people's eyes cannot see. In self-improvement tips, these are things regarding yourselves that you are not aware. Discovering your blinds spots allows you to discover places of improvement or development. It is one of the most important exercises, thus you can use it to discover your individual blind spots.

The relevant exercise helps you to see every person, event or thing that activates you on a given day. An activation means making you feel affected, annoyed, or weird. These will definitely reveal your blind spots.

It is a fun job or exercise because it helps you discover new details about yourself. These new things not only generate benefits but also help you in the self-development skills. Once you identify your blind spots, then try to avoid it. There are different ways present to deal with these blind spots, so you can select the right one as per your individual preferences. The right method helps you change your personality in a positive way, and some other things in an effective way.

5. Quit bad habits

It is vital to determine your bad habits before leaving it. Are there bad activities you can drop? Slouching? Nail biting? Not exercising? Oversleeping? Here are various directions on how you can stop your bad habits. Quitting you bad habits is a critical process because it helps you in your self-development tips. Every habit change provides new possibility. You can recall the healthy benefits you accomplish when you abandon smoking. Once you completely avoid your smoking habit, you will amazingly improve your individual pocket money. The critical benefits always motivate you to start saving. Your habit change not only generates benefits but allows you to improve your personality. To acquire the critical advantage, you can try to identify all the bad habits and stop it immediately. The extraordinary effort helps you hit your personality development goal soon.

6. Compare yourself with really you, not with other people

Some of the people compare their self-improvement skills and earnings with other people to improve themselves, but they fail to realize it because of some reasons. The false comparison process not only impacts your success but destroys your motivation. Instead, you should concentrate on your results and you. The biggest self-improvement technique allows you to perform the process and improve it effectively. Examining your results is important, so you can focus on where you have done wrong things in the earlier period. The important research allows you to avoid the similar missteps in your future. Plus, it appears as a great motivator for people who want to see how much they have improved. Frequently, you can be surprised when you perform an effective review.

7. Meditation

Meditation is the most common and important process that allows you to attain grief from your vital stress and tension. With important features, meditation seems to be a remarkable stress reliever. Not only does meditation generate health benefits but also helps a person avoid anxiety and worry. These are the critical benefits which open your brain of unwanted negative thoughts. This amazing process allows you to feel relaxed and better. If you are meditating properly, you will probably attain these benefits without consuming a lot of time. The great meditation results help you to attain restful sleep and relaxed mind. This is important because it will help you to follow the remaining self-improvement tips

8. Don't fear your failure and take the required break to a lot of fun

You need to learn to redefine your failure as feedback and an accepted size of your successful life. Some people fail once, and lose the motivation. Instead, you need to examine your mistakes properly and attempt to conquer it in your next trial, because regular efforts allow you to accomplish success within the short time duration. Your life is a longtime journey, so you need to make it happier with self-improvement technique. You can consider your failure as a factor to your success because it will inspire you to accomplish your lifetime goal in a successful way.\

Some people do their work in a continuous way to complete their work in a fast way. The wrong working process does not generate the right results. If your car does not have petrol, you cannot drive it. You give yourself a break every week. Self-development is about mastering your requirements to take the right break to relieve your mind. Rejuvenate, relax, and charge yourself for fulfilling your self-improvement goal.

9. Maintain a healthy diet and concentrate on natural resources

A healthy diet plays a critical role in self-development skills process, so you can adhere it well. The right diet allows you to take breakfast or lunch at an apt time. The right intake process allows you to have a healthy lifestyle. You can include simple exercises in your diet process. The correct self-improvement tip generates the right opportunity to have a healthy lifestyle. Along with this, you should wake early in the morning and do simple exercises. You can take fresh vegetables, green leaves, fruits, and some other natural food resources. The correct eating style not only provides you a healthy life but also makes the self-development tips process worthy. But still you can try to eliminate the fast foods and artificially made recipes.

These are simple to follow tips for self-development, so you can follow without any worry. Motivation and self-improvement tips are the effective terms that motivate and inspire you to take part in the self-improvement skills regardless of the challenges.

How to set and achieve goals

Setting goals is one of the amazing tools that you can use to achieve the best state of life. The challenge is, many people don't know how to take advantage of this technique to ensure their goals come true.

In fact, so many people set goals daily, but they never follow through and finally fail to accomplish what they have set out to do. It doesn't matter whether they are life goals, health goals, relationship goals, or spiritual goals, there are ways for setting goals. This section will provide you tips on how to achieve your goals easily.

1. Write down your goals

If you want to learn how to set goals, then you should never underestimate this strategy. When you write down your goals, you are speaking to yourself that you are more dedicated to attain it. Many people will only think about what they want in mind. And the next minute they will forget about their goals. Never allow this to happen to you. If you are serious about fulfilling your goals, put down your goals into writing. Once you write it down, here's the next thing you can do.

2. Share it with 3 people

Whether they are professional goals or personal goals, you need to share your goals with the others so that you make a public commitment to yourself. Well, who should you share your goals with?

The right candidates for this are to select 3 friends or family members whom you know will support you. Don't share your goals with those who will destroy you and say that your goals are impossible to achieve. Go for those who want you to be successful. Choose people who will inspire you and encourage you.

You have to position yourself so that you are dedicated about your goals. If you keep your goals all to yourself and no one realizes about it, it is okay even if you did not act on your goals and fail to realize them. Nobody knows anyway.

3. Read loudly your goals every morning

Every morning the first thing you need to do before you go for work is to read out your goals. You can do this while you are still in the house. Do this regularly, every single day, and don't miss a day for this. You need to program your mind so that your goals are the main focus of your life. You want to make this a habit that you will always remind yourself about your goals, and take action upon them.

Be dedicated to this and do it daily. Programming your goals into your mind is free and it does not consume a lot of your time. Many people have done this and most of them get positive results from this. If reading out your goals every morning can make you successful, just proceed and do it.

4. Examine your goals every week

At the end of every week, you need to cross-examine your goals and your results. What have you attained and where you currently stand. Without understanding your score, you can never know where would be. And if you don't know where you are, it is impossible for you to reach there. Most people set their goals once and they don't review them anymore. That is wrong.

You need to check out your goals at least once a week. Find out whether the actions you did are generating the result you want, else, change your strategy and take action. Sometimes your strategy will have to change as it not generating the results you want.

5. Take a break

Regardless of how dedicated and energetic you feel; you have to take a break at least once a week. You must understand that this isn't a sprint, but a marathon. Nobody will run with the fastest speed and exert all his stamina in a marathon. You don't want to suffer from burnout which may make you breakdown and unable to complete again, unless your goals are super short-term with deadlines within a few days.

Just take a walk in the wood, and set a day for reading, take a short one-day trip, go for sports, and spend good time with your friends and family. Do something that is not related with your goals that will relax your mind and whole body.

6. Learn and improve consistently

If your goal is to become a professional soccer player, learn and improve how to do this consistently. If your goal is to generate money from the stock market, attend seminars, and look for a coach on how to achieve it. Depending on what your goals are, you must learn and improve your skills, your knowledge and your ability so that you can fulfil your goals easily.

All great readers are voracious readers. People read to improve and learn from others. There are books and information present out there to help you fulfill what you want in life. If you need to lose weight, you can join courses and programs to help you. If you want to build a network marketing empire, there are seminars, and a ton of books and courses can help.

7. Implement your goals

This is the secret to doing anything that you want. If you don't do anything, it becomes impossible to get the results you want. Therefore, if you want to become the fastest runner, you must go to the field and practice daily.

When you think about living a great life and accomplishing all the things you want, this is just the first step. When you think about your goals, you will be reflecting them in your mind. You are doing the inner work. But still you need to work on your goals to make them a reality. So don't wait for anything, take action today. Do something to ensure your goals and dreams become a reality.

How to Better Manage Yourself

1. Control your ego

If you look at leadership as an excuse to swan around once you receive accolades for your abilities, then think again. There is humility that comes with great leaders. It is not about you. Leadership is a challenging aspect of motivating others and serving them. Therefore, you must monitor your ego.

2. Your communication

The first thing that you need to learn to control is your listening skills. This is one of the most underrated skill and the one most needed to manage yourself. Simply put, listen and learn. Provide the person in front of you your complete attention.

3. Your trusted network

You must have a coach, a person to challenge you, someone to direct and inspire you and someone who will allow you to see your weakness and strengths. These people can be your colleague, coach, or an official mentor, or a great family friend. Choose wisely and make use of them. Build your network and resist the temptation to tell everybody, everything concerning you.

4. Your emotional state

Leaders must have a mix of warmth and strength. Leaders who lose their emotional cool can be considered as a displaying a lack of strength. This does not mean that you cannot feel strong emotionally, but you need to find a means of dealing with your emotions such that it doesn't make you to spoil in front of your own management. Focus on becoming calm and in control.

5. Your time

Managing your time is important. If you get this wrong, you will have your legs knocked from underneath. You will quickly be overwhelmed. Have some processes and systems in place to control your time, and start the process of educating your team about how and when you will be present-which doesn't need to be all the time.

6. Your focus

As a leader, your concentration will most likely be different results and tasks than your previous role. Although it is tempting to fall into the comfort blanket of carrying out things you are good at, the reality is that you will have new roles. This means a change in the focus and this may drive you from your comfort zone for some time.

7. Your priorities

Set yourself goals and make sure that all your decisions are directed towards achieving them. It is easy to get side-tracked by another person's agenda, and end up with a list of things that don't reflect your priorities.

8. Your levels of energy

Leadership and management roles can be quite demanding, and there could be a habit to burn the midnight oil. No one can work continuously without resting. Take time during the day to leave your desk, spend some five minutes to experience fresh air, and schedule in thinking and planning time, which will be about strategy and delivery of results.

9. Your overall well-being

Get regular exercise, eat well, identify your stressors and develop a support network around you. Know how you react to stress, and what you can do to reduce its effects.

How to conduct successful meetings

For anyone who works in an organization, meetings are a must. And there are different things in corporate life worse than badly chaired meetings. The ones that don't begin on time and don't stay on track but revolve around without any direction, making everyone wonder who is in charge.

But it doesn't have to be that way. A structured meeting that is run well can be effective and productive. Below are strategies that can help chair a meeting.

Send an agenda in advance

An effective meeting requires preparation, and that means setting the agenda. An agenda is the best tool for ensuring your meetings stay on track. It can help you set the right expectations, organize the topics you want to discuss into a great structure, and avoid wasted time.

Send the agenda any critical background material 24 hours early:

Once you have your agenda ready, send it to members for input. There might be something critical that another participant wants to contribute, or something you have forgotten to include-or there are some points you have outlined that are already resolved. By sending the agenda and other materials for other meetings early, you provide people with an opportunity to prepare and make the most of their time.

Highlight critical items in the agenda. Create a list of the highest-priority items, the ones that are most urgent or important. Go through them before you handle the lower-priority items so if something takes longer than planned, you don't have to let the meeting run late.

Find out whether each item on the agenda requires a decision or it can be discussed:

Include both lists as part of the agenda. If possible, apply time limits for all speakers on each agenda item.

Be prepared: For every meeting on your calendar, set aside 15 minutes. Use this time to brainstorm ways you can add value to the meeting. Great preparation will allow you to apply your expertise to the meeting.

Begin on time: If you don't begin your meetings on time, chances are that you won't complete on time. Before you realize, the whole day is consumed on meeting. So you must enforce a strict time rule, and this rules should be followed by everyone in the organization.

Invite the right people: Take time to think about the people who should be present because of their great ideas, expertise, or their need to know. At the same time, don't waste the time of people who should not be there.

Create a parking lot: Whenever the meeting goes off topic but the discussion is good, park the idea to revisit later. And makes sure you really revisit it.

Finish the meeting on time: If you know how to set an agenda with clear results, you will know the time when a meeting should end. Keep in mind that many people have a short concentration span. By having the meeting short and timely, you have a good chance to hold their attention. Time is a great resource, and no one likes when their time is wasted. Optimize meetings as much as you can.

Summarize every agenda item when you complete discussing: Towards the end of the meeting, summarize the next steps that the group has accepted to take. This will make sure that everyone is clear on the tasks that have been assigned to them and the actions they need to take next.

When you master how to lead great meetings, your members will have less wasted time, less frustration, and more time and energy for everyone to complete the work that is important.

Remember that meetings are good if they add value, but if they waste time, get rid of them.

How to become a great team leader?

Learning how to become a great team leader is the most critical skill you must know in your career, especially if you want to reach the corporate ladder. Regardless of how talented you are in your field of expertise; you will never climb through the ranks without a strong management skill.

And yet, there is no single way to the top. The best managers come in all forms, differing in philosophies about employee motivation, team building, and leadership.

Check out these five elements to become a great team leader

1. Get the right talent

Be meticulous as possible in hiring the right people and building an environment where one wants to stay.

If possible, you can use recruiting tools to find the right talent.

If an employee does not work out, the problem can be directed to the interviewing and recruiting process.

Maybe they did not check the references, not enough candidates were screened.

2. Create genuine relationships

This is quite simple. Genuinely care about each of your team members as individuals, and offer them a chance to build their strengths.

To foster for a genuine relationship, start first by caring, and then the rest will follow.

3. Emphasize on visibility

To be a great manager of people and processes in any industry, you must have insight into three aspects:

-What every member of your team is working on.

-The status of projects based on completion.

-The available bandwidth of every individual and your team as a whole.

Without this information, it is hard to get an exact picture of what your team has attained, what they are working on now, or the level of bandwidth for everyone. You won't manage to handle team productivity or predict the future work.

4. Implement expectations regularly

Once you have visibility into team performance, you must be ready to set clear expectations and hold everyone accountable on the team. The biggest distractor to team spirit is when managers let poor productivity or destructive behavior to proceed without action taken.

5. Reward and recognize

Be precise and on time with your compliment. This is the right way to make sure that employee contribution are recognized, and the team feels valued, and productive behaviors are emphasized.

When you recognize excellent behavior, speak about it immediately.

Learning the practices of a good team leader require time and practice. You cannot be motivating and charismatic in overnight. But if you begin by applying these tips into your leadership, you will build a strong leadership foundation.

Chapter 5: Master Time Management

Do you struggle to find time out of the daily hustle of your life? Does your 9-5 work-life consume all your time, or are you pushing all your chores towards the weekend, and then to the next week?

If you have said yes to any of the above questions, then you need to manage your time.

Time management is a critical skill that many people would like to enhance. But they keep stumbling on looking for ways in which they can control time. While there are many strategies for managing time, there are some that work for every situation you experience.

That said, here are the top principles of time management that will allow you to lead a productive life.

1. Planning

Planning is always critical, regardless of what you do. Spend a few minutes in the morning to organize your activities for the day. For a busy schedule, limit distractions as much as you can.

You can still apply different personal planning tools to organize your schedule. Some of these tools comprise wall charts, electronic planners, notebooks, and index cards. List all your tasks and schedules so that you can concentrate on your priorities in your planning tool.

When using a planning tool, factor these things:

- Record all the information on your tool only.
- Make a list of your priorities on the tool and stick to it.
- Make sure you receive a backup system for your planning tool.

- If you are using an electronic device, synchronize it with your computer and recharge the batteries of the planner daily.
- Always walk with your planning tool all the time.

At the end of each workday, spend some minutes to create a list of things to do the following day in your mind. It will mentally record the critical duties on your mind and the less important ones out of your mind on the following day.

2. Organize and Prioritize

Assume your boss has sent you a presentation for the next board meeting and you have only 3-4 days to get ready. The workload is high and you already have various tasks to do. It will be a depressing situation for anyone.

The most important factor of effective time management is distinguishing what is important and what is urgent. Understand that the most critical tasks aren't the most urgent tasks.

The challenge is many of us allow urgent tasks to take over our lives. However, experts say that through both urgent and important tasks can achieve all together, one has to first concentrate on critical ones no matter their urgency. Concentrating on what you want to achieve, will provide you complete control over your time.

If you are completing projects at work, you can apply project management tools such as TimeOn or Trello.

The easiest method to prioritize your tasks is to create a to-do list on a weekly, daily or monthly basis based on your lifestyle. Lis the items in your list depending on priority as high, medium, and low. Implement and mark the highest priorities first.

These tools have critical features to allow you to organize and prioritize your work in terms of importance.

3. The 80/20 Rule

Also known as the Pareto's Principle, the 80/20 rule, when applied to work, means that about 20 per cent of your efforts produce 80 per cent results. So, you should concentrate 20 per cent on making the most effective use of your time.

Identify the most critical tasks and stick to these five steps

- Consider the result you expect.
- Divide it into actions needed to get the job done.

- Perform the action with complete dedication and in the most accurate way.
- Identify and execute the next vital action.
- Repeat until complete.

Apply the 80/20 rule on all tasks listed on your to-do list to increase your efficiency.

4. Do one thing at a time

We all try to do everything at once and up attaining almost nothing. The individuals who try to accomplish many goals at a time were committed and had the least chances to succeed than those who keep themselves focused on a single goal at a time. Successful people focus on one thing at a time as far as possible.

When you try to multitask, the tasks at hand consume more time and we become less productive. As you feel pressured, you begin to think about other unimportant things like what to purchase for the party, arguments with colleagues, etc. lastly, it turns into stress and prevent us from completing our tasks by time and efficiently.

5. Limit distractions

You sit at the desk with the focus to complete a task no matter what. As you press the power on button on your laptop, you discover a friend's message on Facebook or text on your phone and forget about the vital task.

Well, distractions happen, and it is difficult to avoid them. It is challenging to remain focused on a task for hours at a time. However, the practice can assist you to achieve the same.

First, look for internal and external distractor and highlight their cause.

Some tips to help you avoid distractions

- Put down your phone: Regular unscheduled phone calls and messages are common distractions. So turn it off, and forward your work phone to voicemail. Ensure you check your calls after 2-3 hours. Do the same with your inbox.
- Close your web browser: Accept that you are into social media as they are the biggest distractors. Log off your social media profiles and close the screen down.
- Put on headphones: Wear headphones to prevent noise.

- Take a short break. When you feel distracted, take short breaks. These breaks will help you feel relaxed and make your mind clearer.

6. Delegate

Here, you find out tasks that can be done by others and assign those tasks to someone else. It will free up some of your time that you can assign to other core activities. Choose the right persons who can help you by sharing your responsibilities in the best possible way. They should have the right skills, experience, interest and authority to complete the task.

Be clear while setting your expectations. Also, give the person some freedom to personalize the assigned tasks. Ensure you occasionally find out if the person is moving forward and going in the right direction. In a work setting, project management software can be useful for managing teams and making sure everyone is doing well and is headed in the right direction. Lastly, reward the individual for a job well done, or request some changes if needed.

You can also ask others to help you with other important tasks, providing you time to concentrate on critical tasks.

The last thing is to ensure you find the difference between commitment and interest.

7. Live healthy and without stress

How you take care of your body will help you remain healthy physically and mentally. Only people with a healthy mind and body can complete their tasks quickly, and effectively. Practice time management based on your biological clock and schedule important tasks at your peak time of the day.

8. Learn to say "NO"

Unless it is something important, you must learn to refuse some tasks that you think you are pressured. Save that energy and focus to complete activities that are important for you.

If you accept to do everything, you will have a lot of work to do, and soon you will be overwhelmed. This is not right because once you are overwhelmed, you are going to be stressed. So learn to say no to certain tasks.

Chapter 6: Build Self-Confidence

The Art of Self-Acceptance

It is nature as a human being to search for acceptance. People have different goals in life, but many will say that they are seeking happiness. Recent studies have shown that the best path to happiness is to master self-acceptance. However, it is not easy to achieve as one may think.

The power of self-acceptance is important to most people. With family members, society, and friends setting expectations for you, it is not always easy to remain true to yourself and embrace self-acceptance. While accepting yourself for who you are looks simple, it is not that easy for many of us.

Steps to accept yourself

Treat yourself well

Most people are nicer to others than they are to themselves. The power of acceptance means you treat yourself with the same kindness as you treat your best friends and family. Modify the thoughts in your head, if you cannot say those negative things to yourself, then you should not be saying them to yourself.

Everyone has an inner critic voice. This voice tends to undermine our self-esteem and make acceptance of your actions hard.

Be true to yourself

From the start of life, we have been programmed to become responsible people, good students, and a loving brother or sister to our siblings. The pressure starts to develop at an early age to live up to the expectations of others. This shows why it is hard to listen to your inner thoughts that can direct you to your authentic self.

Build a positive support network

If you seek for acceptance and happiness, then you need to surround yourself with positive people. It is easy to fall into relationships without choosing the individuals you want in your life. Family members and work associates are not just hand-picked by you.

All that you need to recall to manage these important relationships is to reduce the time you spend with negative people. If you have family members who pull you down, then you need to decrease your time around them, or in the worst cases, remove them from your life.

Carefully choose friends and partners based on how they make you feel. Do they tear you down or build you up? If you want to stay happy, you need to spend time with people who will make you feel great about yourself. It is as simple as that.

Forgive yourself and others

Everyone has ever made a mistake at one point in life. Don't focus too much on your failures and disappointments in life. You must silence your inner cynic if you want to enjoy life.

Once you stop looking backwards, then you can get ready for an exciting future where you can do well. Take advantage of your strengths and passions so that you can deliver your special gifts to the world and live an orderly life that you were meant to live. Approach your future with a positive attitude, remember to respect who you are and what you want.

Overcoming fear and worry

If you experience fear and worry, use the following steps to calm down and begin to regain control.

1. Take a breath

Probably you may have heard a lot about deep breathing to help reduce anxiety ad worry.

Well, taking a quick, shallow breath is the first activator which awakens other symptoms of anxiety. So when you control your breath, you are able to control other symptoms of anxiety.

If you breathe out longer than you breathe in, your body has to calm right down.

So when you begin to feel fearful:

- Stop
- Concentrate on your breath
- Breathe in to the count of 7

- And slowly breathe out to the count of 11

2. Write down the things you appreciate

Examine the list once you think you are in a bad place.

3. Think of the worst

Try to imagine the worst thing that can happen. After some time, the fear will run away and you chase it.

4. Check the evidence

Sometimes it is useful to challenge the thoughts of fear.

5. Don't try to be perfect

Life is full of stress, yet many of us think that our lives must be perfect. Setbacks and bad days will always happen, and it is important to know that life can be messy.

6. Speak about it

When you share out your fears, it eliminates the worry that might be affecting you.

In summary, the best way to deal with fear is to face it. Escaping it prevents you from moving forward. It makes you worried.

Achieve Total Self Confidence Through a Positive Mental Attitude

1. Positive affirmations

When you speak to yourself, speak positively, regulate your inner dialog. Apply positive affirmations stated in positive, present, and personal tense. Some tips to use include:

- I like myself.
- I can do it.
- I am responsible.
- I feel satisfied.

Approximately 95% of your emotions are defined by the way you talk to yourself as move on with your day. The sad thing is that you if don't consciously speak to yourself in a positive and constructive manner, you will, by default think about the things that make you sad, lower your self-esteem, or make you to worry.

Remember that your mind is like a garden, if you don't take care of it well, weeds will start to grow.

2. Positive people

The kind of people you live with, work, and interact with will have a huge effect on your success and emotions.

Choose today to interact with winners, with people who are happy, and optimistic. With individuals who are headed somewhere in their lives.

Stay away from negative people. Negative people are the main source of life's unhappiness.

3. Positive mental food

The same way your body is healthy to the level which you eat healthy, your mind is healthy to the level which you feed it with "mental protein" instead of "mental candy." Read magazines, books, and articles that are inspirational or motivational.

The point is to feed your mind with positive information and ideas that make you feel happy.

Conclusion

The benefits people and leaders can attain from emotional intelligence are undeniable.

Leaders who are emotionally intelligent create better working environments. This means employees enjoy to work, and feel comfortable to handle risks, as well as suggest the best ideas. Also, they can speak their minds without hurting anyone. In such good environments, collaborative working isn't the only objective, but it is emphasized into the organizational culture.

When a leader is emotionally intelligent, they can apply emotions to move the organization forward. Leaders have the role of effecting any relevant changes in the organization, and if they are aware of others' potential emotional reactions to these changes they can plan the most optimal means to make them.

Additionally, emotionally intelligent leaders don't take things personally and can move forward with plans without worrying the effect on their egos.

Leaders who have a low emotional intelligence tend to burst in stressful situations because they fail to deal with their emotions and this might trigger verbal attacks on others and being passive aggressive.

This can generate an even more stressful environment, where employees are always trying to prevent the next outburst from taking place. This usually causes negative effects on productivity and team cohesion because the employees remain distracted by this fear to concentrate on work and bond.

www.ingramcontent.com/pod-product-compliance
Lightning Source LLC
Chambersburg PA
CBHW070634220526

45466CB00001B/169